Brielle,
   Hope you enjoy this as
much as we did. Your dad
recommended it to us. Gives
you a better picture of our
Father.
          love
          Grampa & Gran

finding the father

HERB MONTGOMERY

See Him for
Who He Really Is

finding
the
father

REVIEW AND HERALD® PUBLISHING ASSOCIATION

Since 1861 | www.reviewandherald.com

Review and Herald® titles may be purchased in bulk for educational, business, fund-raising, or sales promotional use. For information, e-mail SpecialMarkets@reviewandherald.com.

The Review and Herald® Publishing Association publishes biblically based materials for spiritual, physical, and mental growth and Christian discipleship.

The author assumes full responsibility for the accuracy of all facts and quotations as cited in this book.

This book was
Edited by Steven S. Winn
Copyedited by James Cavil
Cover design by Daniel Anez / Review and Herald® Design Center
Cover photo by © Thinkstock.com
Interior design by Johanna Macomber
Typeset: Bembo 11/14

PRINTED IN U.S.A.

15 14 13 12   5 4 3

Unless otherwise noted scripture quotations in this book are from the *New American Standard Bible,* copyright © 1960, 1962, 1963, 1968, 1971, 1972, 1973, 1975, 1977, 1995 by the Lockman Foundation. Used by permission.

Bible texts credited to ASV are from *The Holy Bible,* edited by the American Revision Committee, Standard Edition, Thomas Nelson & Sons, 1901.

Bible texts credited to Basic English are from *The Bible in Basic English.* Copyrighted in the United States by E. P.Dutton & Co., Inc., 1956.

Scripture quotations credited to ESV are from *The Holy Bible,* English Standard Version, copyright © 2001 by Crossway Bibles, a division of Good News Publishers. Used by permission. All rights reserved.

Bible texts credited to KJV are from the King James Version of the Bible.

Texts credited to Message are from *The Message.* Copyright © 1993, 1994, 1995, 1996, 2000, 2001, 2002. Used by permission of NavPress Publishing Group.

Texts credited to MT are from *The Holy Scriptures According to the Masoretic Text: A New Translation,* Jewish Publication Society of America, 1917.

Texts credited to New Jerusalem are from *The New Jerusalem Bible,* copyright © 1985 by Darton, Longman & Todd, Ltd., and Doubleday & Co., Inc. Reprinted by permission of the publisher.

Texts credited to NIV are from the *Holy Bible, New International Version.* Copyright © 1973, 1978, 1984, International Bible Society. Used by permission of Zondervan Bible Publishers.

Texts credited to NKJV are from the New King James Version. Copyright © 1979, 1980, 1982 by Thomas Nelson, Inc. Used by permission. All rights reserved.

Scripture quotations marked NLT are taken from the *Holy Bible,* New Living Translation, copyright © 1996. Used by permission of Tyndale House Publishers, Inc., Wheaton, Illinois 60189. All rights reserved.

Bible texts credited to NRSV are from the New Revised Standard Version of the Bible, copyright © 1989 by the Division of Christian Education of the National Council of the Churches of Christ in the U.S.A. Used by permission.

Texts credited to REB are from *The Revised English Bible.* Copyright © Oxford University Press and Cambridge University Press, 1989. Reprinted by permission.

Bible texts credited to RSV are from the Revised Standard Version of the Bible, copyright © 1946, 1952, 1971, by the Division of Christian Education of the National Council of the Churches of Christ in the U.S.A. Used by permission.

Bible texts credited to TEV are from the *Good News Bible*—Old Testament: Copyright © American Bible Society 1976, 1992; New Testament: Copyright © American Bible Society 1966, 1971, 1976, 1992.

Verses marked TLB are taken from *The Living Bible,* copyright © 1971 by Tyndale House Publishers, Wheaton, Ill. Used by permission.

Texts credited to Young are from *Young's Literal Translation of the Holy Bible* (Grand Rapids: Baker Book House, 1953).

Library of Congress Cataloging-in-Publication Data
Montgomery, Herb, 1975-   .
   Finding the Father : see him for who he really is / Herb Montgomery.
      p. cm.
1. Seventh-Day Adventists–Doctrines. 2. God (Christianity)–Love. I. Title.
   BX6154.M615 2009
   230'.6732—dc22

                                2009022983

ISBN 978-0-8280-2469-3

To my wife, Crystal,
and our children Alexis, Emarya, and Christian,
without whose sacrifice, love, and adoration
I would not have been able to have the ministry I do today.
I know your sacrifice, and I am in awe of you. I love you.

Special thanks to DorAnne Cuenco and Julie Martin,
without whose help these pages would have never seen the light of day.

CONTENTS

INTRODUCTION

We are commissioned by the apostle Paul in his letter to the believers in Ephesus: "Therefore be imitators of God . . . and walk in love" (Eph. 5:1, 2). Today's English Version translates Paul's words, "You must try to be like him. Your life must be controlled by love." *The Revised English Bible* exhorts us to "live in love." *The Message* paraphrases Paul's words, "Watch what God does, and then you do it, like children who learn proper behavior from their parents. Mostly what God does is love you. Keep company with Him and learn a life of love. Observe how Christ loved us. His love was not cautious but extravagant. He didn't love in order to get something from us but to give everything of himself to us. Love like that."

This is what life is truly all about.

Today loving relationships are many times the weakest perceived quality of those who claim to be God's people. We have become more concerned with being correct than being godly, right rather than righteous. Intellectually and behaviorally correct, we have allowed love, both in our understanding of God and as the principle by which we relate to those around us, to wither by the wayside.

I believe this is largely because we have failed to understand, not in our treatment of others, but in our own perception—our own heart-level understanding—what it truly means that God is love. The root of both our misplaced spiritual zeal and our religious malaise is that deep within our hearts we have embraced, silently and subtly, even unknowingly, a wrong picture of God.

God is shining in our hearts (2 Cor. 4:6), hoping that we will understand with our hearts (Isa 6:10). John states, "Everyone who loves . . . knows God. The one who does not love does not know God, for God is love" (1 John 4:7, 8). This is the way Jesus told us we would be able to tell who is really God's and who has yet to truly see Him (John 13:35). How we define God's love and how we reflect that love to those around us is the paramount characteristic that sets His people apart from all others (1 Peter 4:7, 8). Yet how can we imitate that which we do not know or understand? What does it truly mean to believe that God is love? What is love? What does it look like? And once we find it, do we have the courage to truly believe that *that* is what the God of this universe truly is?

That you may fully encounter God's character, that the revelation of Himself would leave not only you but Him with a sense of being overjoyed and overloved, and that you may develop genuine answers to the above questions are the goals of the following pages. His desire is not as much to be in your heart as it is that you would see—and believe—how deeply you are in His. I invite you, dear reader, into a new world, a world of extravagant love, amazing grace, and intimate friendship with the most incredible Being in existence. It is not enough to know that He is love; He would have us understand what that really means. I wish you His best as you enter this new world. May the truths within this small volume usher you from darkness, once and for all, into His marvelous light.

Chapter One

Whom Do You See?

//

"We don't see things as they are. We see things as we are."—Anais Nin.

"You thought I was altogether like you."—God (Psalm 50:21, NKJV).

My first memory in this life took place when I was just 4 years old. I was sitting in one of those 1970s high chairs. You know, the kind with the two metal rods and the stainless steel tray that clamped down into place. Even if a person were raised by an atheist, that sound would trigger an instinctive prayer to God that no body parts were near that thing. There I was, crunching my favorite sugary cereal breakfast with my father sitting to my right and my mother to my left. They were engaged in an argument of such magnitude that it lodged itself in my little 4-year-old heart as my first memory. Ironically, this is the only memory I have of my parents while they were still married.

Before I turned 5, my parents divorced. My mother, almost overnight, became a single mom trying to support and raise a son. To this day I have great respect and love toward my mother for all of the sacrifices I watched her make to raise me. She would drop me off early in the morning at my aunt's house, me in my Superman pajamas (the ones with the enclosed feet—great for sliding across the old hardwood floors), and pick me up in the evening, when I was once again in my pajamas. She worked such long hours that I don't think she ever saw me in normal clothes. She was a hairstylist who worked every day from morning until night, trying to raise a child on minimum wage and tips. Many times those tips determined what we ate for dinner.

What we lacked in money, my mother made up with love. Through the years she and I became fast friends, and to this day she remains one of the best friends I've ever had.

Yet, as I grew closer to my mother, something else was being shaped for me in my heart and mind that I did not know how to put into words. Although my mother was the best mom a child could have and all of the kids in the neighborhood wished they had a mom like mine, from age 4 to age 24 I was forming a picture of this person everyone called my father, shaped by an undercurrent of tension and questions. I remember hearing stories of how my father abandoned *us* for another woman. Whenever I heard that, the *us* didn't seem so plural. My father abandoned *me*. I remember overhearing conversations about my father refusing to pay child support. The hardest thing for my young heart was birthdays and Christmases coming and going without even a card from my dad to say, "Thinking of you, son. Hope you're doing well." What made this most painful was that in our town of only 2,500 people, I actually lived on the same street as my father—only 20 houses away.

When I was 14, I went to visit my father for the first time. The visit was more out of obligation than a real desire to get to know him. I figured, "He's my dad. He helped bring me into this crazy world; the least I could do is pay him a few visits."

I remember standing in my father's kitchen where his wife, out of nowhere, just blurted out, "You know, your father really does love you and wishes you would visit more often." Internally I became livid. My mother had taught me at a very young age when to open my mouth and when to keep it shut. Anger, however, surged through my heart. I wanted so badly to say, "Love? What my dad needs for his birthday is a dictionary. I could define for him what love is, and this is not it!" But I pushed those feelings back down inside.

The years rolled on, and my relationship with my father never seemed to improve. But something unexpected was about to take place, something that would set the course for the rest of my days. When I was 16, I met the girl of my dreams. From the first time I saw her, I knew this was the girl with whom I would spend the rest of my life. What's ironic is that from the first time she saw me, she knew the exact same thing—that I wanted to marry her.

Being a young woman with keen perception, she kept me at arm's distance until we were about 18. After that, things began to get serious. I spent that time jumping from college to college until finally dropping out at 19. I decided to ask her to marry me and arranged for the two of us to meet on the coast in central California, where I had planned to ask the big question.

The evening was perfect. I had made reservations at a beautiful restaurant on the beach, her favorite place. I put unlimited time and effort into creating the perfect atmosphere. I had written her three songs and had purchased some pretty amazing engagement gifts. As the sun was setting, we stood on the rocks and sand of the coast, and I dropped to one knee, took her hand in mine, and . . .

It was at this moment that it dawned on my potential wife what the whole evening was about. Without a moment's hesitation she took her hand out of mine, placed it straight out in front of her, palm facing me, and stopped me dead in my tracks. With world-stand-still sternness, she looked me straight in the eye and said, "Don't even *think* about asking *me* to marry *you!*"

All the hope that had accumulated in my heart since age 16 died. And then, with a twinkle in her eye, she said one word for which I will forever be thankful—"until." Hope revived! I thought to myself, *Until? Until what? When? What's the condition?* I listened intently as she continued: "Until you first have a relationship with your father. Because I'm not going to marry anyone who has a dysfunctional relationship with either one of his parents!"

Talk about compulsory visits with my father! Now I was going to be visiting my father in earnest. Not because I wanted to, but because I had to.

Over the ensuing months I tried diligently to create a relationship with my dad. To be completely honest, our relationship never did click, but it did get to the place where my wife was deceived enough to say "I do." We got married a few months later at age 20, and the polite but distant relationship with my father continued.

One evening, three years later, my wife and I were sitting on the couch in my father's living room, once again in another obligatory visit. My father was seated across from us. The conversation took a drastic twist into uncharted waters, and before I could steer clear, we were right in the middle of the topic I had always feared to broach. My wife was asking most of the questions. If you knew my wife, you would know that she has a way of making people feel so safe and loved that she can ask them any question she wants and, before they know it, they will tell her things they wouldn't even confess to a Catholic priest.

I watched her take my father to a very vulnerable place. Then, with no warning, she went straight for the jugular. Looking my father right in the eyes, she said, "You know, Herb, I don't know how to say what I really want to ask you." She had warmed him up so much that he, in his Southern way, simply came back with "Well, darlin', just come out and say it." That's all she needed. Quietly but firmly she continued, "I'd like to know why you didn't visit your son more often when he was a little boy."

Talk about an obligatory discussion! Everything inside me was screaming at my wife, "Hello! I'm sitting right here! I'm in the room! What are you doing?" I tried to shoot my wife "the look," but she was oblivious. My father was shocked as well. He didn't know what to say. His body language displayed his discomfort. He crossed his arms, uncrossed them, and crossed them again. Having nowhere to hide, nowhere to run, he looked at me and said, "Stanley [my middle name, since I'm a second], I know you love your mother very much, and I would hate to do anything that would interfere with that, but I think it's time you knew something." Then he leaned over, looked into my eyes, and said words that I had never heard before.

"When I left your mother . . ." he started. My mind jolted. I thought to myself, *My mother? No, dad. You abandoned* me! My father continued: ". . . I never, in my wildest imagination, even conceived of the thought that I would lose you."

Tears began to well up in my father's eyes as he went on to tell the story of a very heated and lengthy custody battle that granted my mother custody and permitted my father visits only on the weekends. But in spite of the court order, my father would never be allowed to see his son. I had always been told that my father didn't want to see me on the weekends. Now I was hearing, for the first time, of the countless efforts my father made to try to see me, and how those efforts were circumvented and prevented by my mother. I began to realize that our move to another state during my childhood had not occurred because of my mother's work, as I had been told, but to prevent my father from seeing me.

My father stood up and motioned for me to follow him into the dining room. He proceeded to open a drawer in a huge antique cabinet, and pulled out what looked to me like an old shoebox. As he lifted the lid, there, filed in chronological order, was a sight I will never forget.

Every child support check, processed through my mother's bank account and returned with my father's monthly bank statement, was there staring right back at me. Sometimes they were early and written for more than what was required. "I always *tried* to take care of you," my father whispered.

Then, looking up into his eyes, I watched him proceed very cautiously. Not wanting to cause discord between me and my mother, but still desiring for me to know the truth, he told of birthday presents that were thrown away by my mother or returned to him with nothing more on the package than "return to sender."

I sat there speechless, not knowing what to believe. Then, for the first time, I heard of the countless prayers that my father had prayed that someday I would come to know the truth.

In that moment something inside of me broke, and tears began to well up in my eyes. I looked up and saw tears streaming down my father's face as well. It was hard for me to swallow. My mind raced back over all my years of feeling abandoned by my father, all the suppressed emotional pain of watching other young boys playing at the park with their dads and wondering, *What's wrong with me?* All the pain of feeling rejected by *my* father burst upon my 4-year-old little heart trapped in my 23-year-old body. My father very cautiously reached out and took his me in his arms. I couldn't hold it back any longer. After all the years of feeling abandoned, I found myself in the embrace of the father I had always wished I had. With tears streaming down both of our faces, I, *for the first time in my life,* at 23, *loved* my dad. What I would begin to realize next would change every aspect of my life.

Chapter Two

A New Paradigm

"Man is fed with fables through life, and leaves it in the belief he knows something of what has been passing, when in truth he has known nothing but what has passed under his own eye."—THOMAS JEFFERSON.

I remember hearing of a story about a father riding a subway car with his four young children. These children were, most assuredly, the type of children that would make you never want to have kids. As the father was sitting, engrossed in thought, his children were quite the opposite. One was incessantly pulling on the tie of a nicely dressed man as he was trying to hold an important conversation on his cell phone. Another was running up and down the middle aisle screaming at the top of her lungs. The third was sitting near a conservatively dressed woman, asking questions that would make even a sailor blush. The fourth child, however, took the prize. He was literally balancing himself on the headrest of one of the seats, shining the bald head of a passenger.

The entire car was about to explode when one of the passengers worked up the courage to approach the father. In a gruff tone he blurted out, "Can't you see what your children are doing? What kind of a father are you?" (Have you ever noticed that you can become immune to the behavior of your children and not even notice what they are doing?) As if to notice for the first time what his children were doing, the father snapped back into reality. He looked up at his fellow passenger as tears began to fill his eyes. Overcome by the emotion of the events he faced in his life, he spoke softly, "Oh, I am so sorry. You see, we have just returned from the hospital where these children just lost their mother and I my wife, and I guess we are all just dealing with it the best way we know how." The whole subway car fell silent.

Were the children still bouncing off the walls of the subway car? Yes.

But were they still simply the most unruly children these passengers had ever met, or had more information about their situation caused a shift in the way they *viewed* the children? No longer were they out of control; they were now children dealing with the recent loss of their mother in the best way they knew how. The change was not in the behavior of the children but in the way the passengers *looked* at their behavior. The facts of the situation did not change, but the way those passengers *viewed* those facts did. What you, dear reader, and the passengers on that subway car just went through was what I went through with my father and what I was about to go through with God. I experienced a paradigm shift.

Paradigms are not the facts that surround us, but the way we *look* at those facts. Our paradigms are not the world around us, but the way we *look* at the world around us. An example of this can be seen in the way many people relate to the Old Testament. Some see the God of the Old Testament as a bloodthirsty tyrant, while others, reading the same stories, see a God of love. The facts of those Old Testament stories are the same, but the way these two groups view the facts is as different as day and night.

Our personal paradigms can be seen as our maps of our surroundings in life. When we look at a map, we are looking, not at the actual streets, but at someone's interpretation of the actual streets. We judge the accuracy of a map by how closely its interpretation of the territory matches the actual territory. In the same way, our paradigms are not reality, but the way we view what is real. We can judge the accuracy of our paradigm only by how closely it matches reality.

One day a close friend of mine and I were sharing our faith door to door. He had visited a family the day before and was going back for a second visit, but this time we were having a difficult time finding their home. We drove around for hours, and finally, exasperated, he flipped over the map and realized that he had been looking not only at a map of a different county but of an entirely different state! (In moments like these you can either laugh or cry, so we laughed.)

Put yourself in this story. What would you have done during those two hours? In retrospect, the solution seems obvious, but while we were going through it we felt as if we simply needed to try harder. But this is just the point. The problem wasn't that we were not trying hard enough—the problem was that we had the wrong map!

This accurately illustrates why many of us get frustrated in our religious experience. When we run into difficulties, many of us focus on our behavior and decide that we need to put in more effort. Others stick out their chin and decide to have a positive attitude, saying such things as "After all, happiness is a choice." But I want you to stop and consider these options in light of the experience my friend and I had with the map. We could have put in more effort. As a matter of fact, we did, and the only result was more frustration. We could have worked on our attitudes, but no matter how positive we may have been, in the end we would only have been positively lost. The problem was not a lack of effort or a negative attitude. The problem was the map!

I had a wrong paradigm of my father. What I went through with my dad was a paradigm shift. The facts of the custody battle, the birthday gifts, missed visits, and child support payments did not change. Rather, the way I *saw these things* did!

Stop and consider. Your parents may still be happily married. Your earthly family may not have gone through anything like mine. Yet my story is not mine alone. It is the story of every one of you reading this book. Since our birth we have been raised in a world in which our culture, our churches, and our families have been whispering lies to us about our *heavenly* Father. I don't believe anyone did this to us with malicious intent, but we have been lied to nonetheless.

In our religious experience, as in the story of the map, many of us are putting in more and more effort, getting back few results, and ending up completely frustrated. The solution is not in focusing on our behavior, nor is the solution in simply having a positive attitude while settling for a stale religious experience. The solution is to go through a radical change in our religious map, the way we *see* God, and experience a spiritual *paradigm* shift.

Ninety-nine percent of all the sermons we listen to, books we read, and quotations we underline deal in the realm of behavior and attitude. It's no wonder many of us feel as if we are getting nowhere. I would like to suggest that as long as we focus on our own effort, placing our attention on behavioral conformity and attitude adjustments alone, the solution to our spiritual frustration will always elude us. Let me explain.

Remember the subway car story? Follow the path closely from cause to effect. With the new information, the passengers *saw* those unfortunate children differently, which caused them to *think* about them differently, which caused them to *feel* differently toward them, which changed their *behavior* and *attitude*. How we *see* determines how we *think*. How we *think* determines how we *feel*. And how we *feel* determines our *behaviors* and *attitudes* and thus our *experience*. The problem lies not in our behavior but in our map, our paradigm, the way we *see*.

Today's religions, whether Buddhist, Hindu, Muslim, Jewish, or Christian, focus largely on their adherents' *behavior*. As long as we continue to focus on our behavior, our *experience* will never change. What we desperately need is a change in how we *see* God, our paradigms of His thoughts and feelings toward us.

In my short life I have met many people who say that they used to be Christians. I ask why, and remarkably, it often boils down to the same thing. They get frustrated by their inability to live up to the expectations of other Christians. Today they believe that Christianity is a joke. They view God as stern and against them, or at the very least as someone who is never satisfied. I would like to suggest that the problem is not Christianity, but the way we, as Christians, *see* God. Jesus explained it this way:

"It is the spirit that quickeneth; the flesh profiteth nothing: the words that I speak unto you, they are spirit, and they are life" (John 6:63, KJV).

Here Jesus makes a profound statement. What every person wants, whether he or she knows it or not, is a viable, dynamic, spiritual experience with God. This is the purpose of his or her existence. We were not made simply to think, but to feel. Jesus states very clearly that it is the spirit that gives life to the spiritual dimension of our existence. Now, follow His words carefully. He said that the flesh profits nothing. The flesh could be summed up as *our* attempt to put forth more effort, our decision to have a more positive attitude, or our focus on our behavior. But Jesus said that these profit nothing. What we need is the spirit, and how He defines this spirit is revolutionary.

Jesus is referring to the story of creation. Adam was simply a dirt sculpture into whom God breathed the spirit of life. It wasn't the dirt that brought him to life, but the spirit! What is this spirit that gives life to us *spiritually* when God breathes it into us? Jesus is not talking about the Holy Spirit, because He said, "The *words* that I speak unto you, *they* are spirit, *they* are life."

Words? What does He mean by words? Words are very powerful things. They communicate ideas, thoughts, and they even have the power to change paradigms. Look carefully at Jesus' words. What were His words about? Or rather, *whom* were they about? A casual afternoon reading of Jesus' parables reveal that they were about "the kingdom of heaven." It seems as though every time Jesus opened His mouth, His very first words were "The kingdom of heaven is like . . ."

When someone says, "I don't like the way city hall does things!" what is that person talking about? Not the bricks and mortar of the building, but the people who govern there and their policies. When Jesus said, "The kingdom of heaven is like . . . ," He wasn't talking about what the streets are made of or how big the mansions are, but rather what the person who governs there is like!

Jesus' teachings were neither pep talks, trying to squeeze out more stringent behavior or more effort, nor popular self-help speeches on how to have a positive attitude. Rather, Jesus was concerned primarily with how we *see* the person ruling the kingdom of heaven. His goal was to correct how we *view* God. Jesus knew that a call for more effort, a demand for a change in our attitude, or a lecture about our behavior, while leaving our corrupt pictures of God intact, would produce only frustration.

So he began with the solution. He sought to correct our *map*, our perception of God, by saying in effect: "Listen, more self-dependent effort will profit you nothing. You need to have the way you see God radically changed. A correct understanding of God will infuse your experience with the power and life that you so desperately desire. Just as it was the Spirit that gave life to Adam physically, My teachings about God are spirit and they are life for you spiritually."

Have you ever felt as if your relationship with God depended on you, while the more effort you put in, the harder it got? Or have you ever put more effort into your relationship with God only to get back more frustration? Has your relationship with God ever been like a proverbial carrot hanging out in front of you, just beyond your grasp? Have you ever felt as if your prayers didn't even make it past the ceiling? If so, you are not alone.

What you need, dear reader, is a radical change in your paradigm of God. A radical change in the way you view God will bring with it a radical change in your thoughts toward God. The change in your thoughts toward God will bring about a change in the way you feel toward God. Finally, the change in your thoughts and feelings toward God will bring about a change in your behavior, your attitude, and eventually your experience as a whole. The change that you long to experience in your behavior does not come through more effort. It comes through a change in how you *see*. Look closely at the following illustration:

Character

| Seeing | **Determines** → | Thoughts and Feelings | **Determines** → | Behaviors, Attitudes, Experience |

In our religious experience, change in behavior is *not* the result of a strong will or more decided effort. It is the result of a change in how we *see*. Do you long for a change? Do you long to have a living, dynamic spiritual experience with God? Embark with me, then, on a journey of change. Not just in behavior or attitude, but in perception. You see, character is revealed through actions. And character, by definition, is comprised of an individual's thoughts and feelings. But a person's thoughts and feelings are determined by his perceptions.

This all works in reverse, as well. As we study God's actions toward the human race, His ultimate desire is that we would see beyond His actions to the thoughts and feelings in His heart toward us that lead to His actions. His hope is that we would perceive something of the love that surges in His heart for us, that compels His actions of kindness toward us. He longs for us to see the way He *sees* us.

Therefore, I invite you, through the remaining pages of this book, to step into the realm of Amazing Grace, Extravagant Love, and Intimate Friendship. It is in these themes alone that we find the change for which we long. We focus so much on behavior, but what would happen if we prayed for a dynamic change in our picture of God? Could it be that we are wishing for a *heavenly* Daddy to love and who loves us? Are we struggling to have a relationship with Him, wishing that it were alive and meaningful, but not recognizing the real root of our frustration—our wrong perception of Him? May your prayer throughout the remainder of this book be just like that of blind Bartimaeus: "Son of David, I just want to see."[1] This is the eye salve we so desperately need.[2] Do you want it, my friend? Then come with me quickly to what we need to *see* first.

FINDING THE FATHER

[1] "When he heard that it was Jesus the Nazarene, he began to cry out and say, 'Jesus, Son of David, have mercy on me!' Many were sternly telling him to be quiet, but he kept crying out all the more, 'Son of David, have mercy on me!' And Jesus stopped and said, 'Call him here.' So they called the blind man, saying to him, 'Take courage, stand up! He is calling for you.' Throwing aside his cloak, he jumped up and came to Jesus. And answering him, Jesus said, 'What do you want Me to do for you?' And the blind man said to Him, 'Rabboni, I want to regain my sight!' And Jesus said to him, 'Go; your faith has made you well.' Immediately he regained his sight and began following Him on the road" (Mark 10:47-52)..

[2] "I advise you to buy from Me gold refined by fire so that you may become rich, and white garments so that you may clothe yourself, and that the shame of your nakedness will not be revealed; and eye salve to anoint your eyes so that you may see" (Rev. 3:18).

Chapter Three

Eternal Longings

///

"If I find in myself a desire which no experience in this world can satisfy, the most probable explanation is that I was made for another world."—C. S. LEWIS.

"You who in heart long for something better than this world can give recognize this longing as the voice of God to your soul."—E. G. WHITE.

Have you ever felt haunted by a deep heart-longing for something more fulfilling, more meaningful, or simply more satisfying? Yet if someone asked you, would you be able to discern what it was that you really desired? I have experienced that longing too, and like many others, it has happened too many times to mention. The story of my life is strewn with my personal attempts to satisfy an ever-present aching hunger in my heart.

As I look back, one thing becomes painfully clear. The many attempts in my past to satiate my heart's hunger have always been just that—attempts. Each vain pursuit was short-lived, leaving my soul's thirst unquenched and in greater want than at the start. My own personal journey has left me with two heart-searching questions. First: "What is this longing that seems to be part of the very fabric of my being?" And the second: "What is it that I really desire?"

In my search for answers, I've been surprised to find that in my eternal, never-fully-satisfied longings, I am not alone. Growing up on the media of MTV and VH1, I remember Mick Jagger's lyrics, "I can't get no satisfaction." In the 1980s Bono sang the words, "I still haven't found what I'm looking for." A few years ago Switchfoot, a group at the top of the charts at the time, was singing, "We were meant to live for so much more!" (While contemporary poets and prophets can't provide a solution, they very often place their finger on the pulse of the problem.)

Surprisingly King David shared these sentiments as well. At the height of his political success, King David penned the words, "My soul thirsts . . . my flesh yearns . . . in a dry and weary land where there is no water."[1] Growing up, I remember hearing countless times that if I could have just three things I would be happy: money, power, and sex. What is surprising is that King David had money, he had power, and he even had women in his life, but he realized that his heart was thirsting for what he could not find. And here is the most shocking realization: David had the audacity to identify the object of his thirst . . . God.

To be honest, when I first realized this, I questioned whether David really meant what he wrote. Was he just trying to be pious? So many times we say what we are supposed to say rather than what we are really feeling. But the more I pondered David's statement, the more I questioned, Have I missed something? Could this longing in my heart really be a longing for intimacy with God? Why was my heart so averse to this? Is there something unfulfilling about God, or is the real problem similar to what I had encountered with my dad? Maybe I just didn't see Him as He really is. Could I have the wrong picture of this God with whom I was trying to have a relationship?

I found myself in a world of doubt. Nothing I had ever heard about God was appealing, much less deeply satisfying. Then I stumbled on other statements that caught my attention. "You open Your hand and satisfy the *desire* of every living thing" (Ps. 145:16). "In Your *presence* is *fullness* of joy; in Your right hand there are *pleasures* forever" (Ps. 16:11). At this point I had to come to a conclusion. Either these verses were just foolish notions, or maybe, in all the time I'd been a Christian, I had never really encountered God as He really is. I chose the second option, and embarked on a journey of discovery—a quest of seeing and believing, a journey of epic dimensions in my heart and life. I fell to my knees with one prayer: "Dear Lord, help me to understand You, not merely on an intellectual level, but help me to see You with my *heart*."[2] I came to the conclusion that I had erred in my heart. I knew a lot of doctrine. I was well versed in the standards and lifestyle of a devout Christian. Yet, as religious as I may have been, on a heart level I had been blind to the "ways" of God.[3] Could this be why my heart felt so empty? I wondered and prayed, "Lord, what am I missing in my religious experience?"

Dear reader, I want to ask your permission to take you on a journey of discovery—a discovery of epic dimensions for your heart and life, a journey of encountering things concerning our God that have lain hidden since the days of the apostles who whisper to us, "There's more; just look closely."

As we continue through this chapter, several pages from now you are going to be wondering where all this is headed. Please keep holding on. You are about to encounter the puzzle pieces of one of the most incredible pictures of God in all of the Scriptures. You are about to discover what God has longed for you to experience from the very dawn of time.

Let's start with the words of Isaiah, "Then I heard the voice of the Lord, saying, 'Whom shall I send, and who will go for Us?' Then I said, 'Here am I. Send me!'" (Isa. 6:8, NASB). It is paramount that we pay close attention to the language here. Isaiah hears the Lord referring to Himself in the singular term "I."

This seems logical, because "The Lord our God is one."[4] Yet watch the change that takes place in God's simple question—a sudden change from the singular "I" to the plural "Us." What difference does that make?

As I pondered this verse the first time, I thought, *OK, God, I am going to trust that I have misunderstood something about You that is keeping my heart at bay. What is it? What are You trying to show me about Yourself in this verse?* Then the light began to dawn. Jesus, when speaking of God, referred to a "Father," "Son," and "Holy Spirit."[5] Paul, too, wrote of "Jesus," "God," and the "Holy Spirit."[6]

Then the lights began to shine brighter. The apostle John stated that God is, by nature, the very essence of love.[7] What is love? Did God create love? The more I pondered, the clearer it became. Love is not something God created—love is what He *is*. He has always been love, and He will always be love. Just as God has no beginning, neither does love, which is the essence of His existence.

Let me take you on a related tangent. On the sixth day of Creation, Moses records God as saying, "It is not good for the man to be alone" (Gen. 2:18). But why? Why was it not good for Adam to be alone? Was there something wrong with the way humanity was made? ("Don't leave that guy all by himself.") Or is there something in the nature of being alone that, in itself, is not good? Are there things that, by their very nature, are impossible to experience if one is all by oneself?

The best example of this is tickling. Yep, that's right. Have you ever tried to tickle yourself? It's impossible! Try it sometime. In order to experience the full sensation of being tickled, more than one person must be involved.

Besides having your back scratched in certain places, having a staring contest, and being tickled, the single most significant experience one cannot have all by oneself is a relationship based on love. Someone may object, saying, "You can scratch your own back with a backscratcher. With a mirror you could have a staring contest with yourself. The tickling, well, you've got me there, but you *can* love yourself!"

Now, I agree that we need to have a healthy sense of self-respect. But when it comes to love, let me simply say this. Love, by definition, is other-centeredness. It is something that begins in you and ends in someone or something else. If what you are feeling begins with you and ends with you, *please* call it something else, like self-esteem, self-respect, or self-confidence, but don't call it love. In order for it to exist, love requires more than one person between whom its ebb and flow occurs.

Now, saying all this, and knowing that it is not good for humans to be alone, do you think it is good for even God to be alone? Was He ever alone? Has God always been an "Us"?

You see, although we cannot understand it, the Bible teaches that God has always been. Since God has always been, and God is love, then love has always been. Remember, love is not something God created, or else it would have a beginning. Love is what God is, and just as you cannot give a reason for the existence of God, you also cannot give a reason for the existence of His love.

When my wife and I were dating, many times she would ask me the famous question that two young people in love so often ask: "Why do you love me?" And it would stump me. If I gave a reason that I loved her, what would happen if that reason failed? What if I said it was because of looks? (Wrong thing ever to say to a woman, by the way.) What would happen if, as she got older, her looks went out the window? Suppose I said I loved her because she was such a nice person or because of her winning personality. What if one day she became really grouchy or dull? What if I said that I loved her because of her upright character? What would happen if my wife fell into a moral failure? If any of the above reasons failed, would that mean that my love, being based on those reasons, would also fail? The Bible says true love "never fails."[8] Therefore, being able to give a *reason* for loving someone proves that your love is not genuine. For if that reason would ever fail, then your love would fail, and true love *never* fails.

Then it dawned on me that love is its own reason. When looking for a reason for the basis of love, we must be content simply to say that "love loves." Love loves because it is love. (I must admit she didn't like that answer very much. I think she was looking for something more romantic and less logical.)

Why do we spend countless hours and endless effort seeking to create reasons God loves us? We fall into the deception that God's love is based on something in us, either our behavior or what we believe. Could it be that God is good to us, not because we are good, but because He is good? Could it be that God is nice to us, not because we are nice, but because He is nice? Maybe God loves us because He is love, and that's just what love does. Love loves.

Since love is other-centered (requiring the presence of more than one for its existence), and love has always been (for God is love), it is only logical that more than one being has always existed between whom love has ebbed and flowed. Jesus gives us insight into the identity of these Beings. Matthew records that Jesus commissioned us to baptize "in the name of the Father and the Son and the Holy Spirit" (Matt. 28:19). Also, Paul speaks of "The grace of the Lord Jesus Christ, and the love of God, and the fellowship of the Holy Spirit" (2 Cor. 13:14). They are three and yet simultaneously one.

This "three in one" union is not for the purpose of taking care of some synergistic cosmic business in which they can accomplish more together than apart. Nor is the nature of their union a business model in which they simply pool their resources. Rather, it is a union of love. It's the same type of union that makes pluralities on earth a single unit. Notice how Moses put it when writing of Creation: "For this reason a man shall leave his father and his mother, and be joined to his wife; and *they* shall become *one* flesh" (Gen. 2:24). Did you catch that? Even though a man and a woman may be two individuals with separate identities, at the same time love makes them one. God *is* love, and that which exists and flows between Father, Son, and Holy Ghost is love. That is why being three, They are yet one.

Imagine what it must have been like for the three of Them from eternity past, before any act of creation. To do that, you need to imagine what life would be like if you were married to the most unselfish person on the planet. I have asked for one-word answers from many audiences, and the responses are always similar: "happiness," "pleasure," "love," "peace," "joy," "fulfilling," "wonderful," "heaven." But my all-time favorite answer is "existential bliss."

Love is ever–deepening. Have you ever had someone do something really nice for you? What did it awaken in you toward them in return? That's right. You wanted to do something nice for them. Then what does that make them want to do? Well, it makes them want to do something nice for you again, which makes you want to do something even nicer for them, which makes them want to do something even nicer for you! And so kindness, an expression of love, has the potential to continually deepen. Have you ever been in a relationship in which the more you were loved, the more you wanted to love in return?

I travel for most of the weekends throughout the year, so during the week, my oldest daughter always wants me to tuck her into bed at night. I read her a story, pray with her, talk with her about her day, get her a drink of water—all the good stuff! One night, as I turned out the lights and was about to shut the door, she said, "Papa?"

"Yes, dear," I responded.

"I love you more than the angels can love."

My heart melted. I assured her that I loved her even more, and we said good night.

The next morning, sitting at the breakfast table, I asked her whether she had heard that phrase somewhere or whether she had made it up herself. She said, "No, Pop, I made that up myself." I pressed her for what she meant by it, and in her little 7-year-old reasoning, this is what she told me. "I know I can't love you as much as God loves you, but I'm pretty sure I love you more than the angels do."

Well, up to this point I was touched by the pure poetic nature of her words, but then I began to see what was really taking place in her heart. She wasn't trying to be poetic—she was experiencing the ever-deepening nature of love. The more I loved her, the more she loved me. This, in turn, caused me to express my love to her even more, which caused her love to deepen along with her desire to express her love to me in a greater way. And now she had reached what, in her mind, was the ceiling. The only being in the world that she conceived could love her papa more than she did was God and God alone.

Now take this principle and apply it to the three-in-one God. Think back, once again, to before any act of creation was done. The Father loved the Son and the Spirit. The Son loved the Father and the Spirit. The Spirit loved the Father and the Son. The more They expressed their love to one another, the deeper the love, the stronger the emotions, the deeper the devotion, until they were in the heightened state of what others have named "existential bliss." They were experiencing the ever-deepening existential pleasure of pure unselfish love. Imagine the pleasure like steam in a pressure cooker. The pleasure builds and builds as the love persistently deepens. Then what? What happens next?

In order to answer that, I would like you to consider one more thought. Have you ever tasted really good food? I mean the really good stuff. The moment the first bite touches your taste buds, what is the first thing (besides getting more) that you want to do? After a religious presentation I gave to an audience of young people, a young woman came up to me so excited that she just had to share something with me. With one hand behind her back, she extended to me with the other hand, of all things, a potato chip. She said, "Just close your eyes and open your mouth." So, being the trusting person I am, I obeyed.

It had been a long time since I had tasted anything that disgusting. I opened my eyes and realized from the expectant expression on her face that she really liked these particular potato chips. And so, with all the kindness I could muster, I swallowed and said, "Uh, what flavor is that potato chip?" Without hesitation she withdrew her other hand from behind her back to reveal a *ketchup*-flavored bag of Lays potato chips. On the bag, scripted in red letters, was written, "No one can eat just one." I remember wishing I hadn't even done that! Then I carefully broke the news to her that, although she thought they were delicious, these potato chips were the worst I had ever tasted. I guess pleasure is in the taste buds of the taster. But I hated them just the same. (Wendy, if you're reading this, um, they're still the worst.)

She was experiencing immense pleasure, and her first and only impulse was to immediately share it with someone else. I'm sure we've all experienced this. We experience something really amazing, and the next thing coming out of our mouth, as we lean over to the person next to us, is "Hey, you gotta check this out!"

Now apply this universal principle to the Godhead, and let's put the whole picture together. Imagine the Father loving the Son and the Spirit, the Spirit loving the Father and the Son, and the Son loving the Father and the Spirit. Upon each expression, their love is deepening, and so is the joy and pleasure of being in such a fresh, unselfish relationship. They are continually experiencing the bliss of loving completely while simultaneously being loved. Then in the midst of this love, they begin to desire to share this bliss, but there's a problem. They are the only ones in existence. No other beings have yet been created.

Here is what I believe to have been the primary motive in God's creation of the universe. Creation was not because God was lonely, in need of worship, or desirous of servants to do the things with which They did not want to dirty their hands. There was not a single iota of selfish impulse or self-centered motive involved in God's desire to bring other beings into existence. Rather, God was moved by a purely unselfish motive simply to share the love that They had been experiencing throughout the boundless ages of eternity. How do we know this? Pay careful attention to the following statement by Moses: "Then God said, 'Let *Us* make *man* in *Our* image, according to *Our* likeness; and let *them* rule. . . .' God created *man* in His own image, in the image of God He created him; male and female He created *them*" (Gen. 1:26, 27).

There are a few things we need to notice in this text. First, God is, again, speaking in the plural form as an *Us,* and referring to a plural likeness as *Our* likeness. What exactly was this likeness? They were three existing in the form of the oneness of love—a singular plurality, as some have said. But remember what it is that makes a plurality of individuals into a singular unit. It's love.

Second, we cannot afford to miss the point that when God said, "Let us make *man* . . . ," man here is also plural. God did not intend to create a single human being in the image of God. This would, in its truest definition, be impossible. God never was a single being, and neither could this triune love exist and be experienced by Adam all by himself. And so God's intent from the very beginning was to create not simply one individual but a human singular plurality that would exist in a relationship of love—loving each other, while simultaneously being loved by each other. God was experiencing the bliss of love to such a degree that He wanted to create others who, although they would be separate individuals, would exist in the singular plurality of love, sharing in God's experience of loving while being loved—being two, yet also simultaneously being one. "For this reason a man shall leave his father and his mother, and be joined to his wife; and *they* [a plurality] shall become *one flesh* [a singularity]" (Gen. 2:24).

You see, none of us is an image of God while we exist as an isolated person on an island from the rest of society. God is not just one individual, but Three, in a oneness of love. Therefore, for any of us to be restored to God's image, we must also be a plurality of individuals existing in a relationship of love that makes us one. Then the image of what God really is becomes reproduced. This means that we are not going to get there all by ourselves. It requires more than one individual for the image of God to be reproduced. It requires, at the very least, two individuals who must be living in that oneness of love. They must become a singular plurality themselves. We were meant to live in relationship with others either as husband and wife, or as a family, or as a church family. Stop here and imagine what church would be like if this were truly understood.

Notice Jesus' prayer for His church just before His crucifixion. "The glory which You have given Me I have given to them, that *they may be one, just as We are one*" (John 17:22). This is truly an amazing statement. The oneness that exists between the Father, Son, and Holy Ghost is not some hard-to-understand subject dealing with physiology. They are one because of the love that flows between them. Jesus takes this union of love and prays that believers would experience together, among themselves, exactly the same union, the same love, that makes the Godhead one—that we, through love, would be one together as believers, just as the Father, Son, and Holy Ghost are one. Could it be that I had missed the entire central emphasis of what God meant for my spiritual life to look like?

"I pray also for those who will believe in me through their message, that *all of them may be one*, Father, *just as you are in me and I am in you*. May they also be in us so that" "*they may be one as we are one*" (verses 20-22, NIV). "I in them and You in Me, that they may be perfected in unity, so that the world may know that You sent Me, and loved them, even as You have loved Me. Father, I desire that they also, whom You have given Me, be with Me where I am. . . . O righteous Father, although the world has not known You, yet I have known You" (versus 23-25). "I have made You known to them, and will continue to make You known in order that *the love You have for Me may be in them* and that I Myself may be in them" (verse 26, NIV). Again, none of us is going to answer this prayer alone.

It has always been God's desire, and still is today, that we would be able to experience the same love They experience, this love of being individuals but singularly one through love.

And so we are left with an alarming conclusion. We were made for love. Maybe all the longings we each experience for something more, something just beyond our grasp, are the longings to return to that for which we were made—to love and be loved.

Every one of us longs for this. Not one person escapes this eternal longing. Whether we recognize this longing as a hunger to love and be loved or not, it still remains the same. We may confuse it as a need for money, power, or sex, but it is actually a longing for love. All other pursuits are ultimately empty and leave us hungering. But love satisfies. It quenches.

Take family, for example. When looking at marriage from the viewpoint of how much a person gives up, there is a lot of sacrifice that one must willingly embrace for a marriage to function. And then when you add children to the mix, the sacrifice becomes enormous. When you look at family from a modern, materialistic point of view, it really does not make much logical sense to choose to get married, have children, and live the next 30 years sacrificing yourself for the benefit of this unit. But when we look at it from the viewpoint of our eternal longing to love and be loved, we immediately begin to see why human beings consistently choose to spend the rest of their lives with another and then choose willingly and joyously to engage in bringing up children. It's all for love. The human desire to have a family is proof positive that we will give up *anything* for the possibility of experiencing the phenomenon of loving another while simultaneously being loved. In these relationships we sense the echoes of Eden, a faint whisper saying, "This is why you were made." It is why we are here.

We all long for love above all else, and nothing short of it will ever make any one of us feel fully satisfied. Ultimately, all of these longings are, as we saw at the beginning of this chapter, satisfied by God Himself, for "God is love" (1 John 4:8). Many of us fail to realize that we get the love that we all so desperately long for, not from others, but "from God" (verse 7). God is much more than religious doctrines or moral regulations. God is love!

It is always amazing to me how many people do not show up for a weekend seminar that has been advertised as being on the topic of God's love. For prophecy or end-time events, the crowd is a little larger. But if I advertised a seminar in today's culture about financial wealth and debt-free living, saying, "I'll give you five easy steps to have any material possession you desire and still live a debt-free life," tons of people would show up. And, if I said the seminar was free, even more would show up. We think money will satisfy that longing inside of us, but studies have shown that financial affluence, after meeting a certain level of needs, does not make a person happier. While their money grows, their happiness levels remain the same.[9]

Something else that people think will satisfy their deep heart longings is a perverted version of sex, or lust. Studies show that even among pastors and religious leaders, the abuses of sex are being imbibed through the Internet. But will sex without the foundations of love and relationship satisfy our deep heart longings?

In comparison, God and His great love for humanity as the center and source of all our happiness and fulfillment attracts minimal attention. We hear the word "God," and immediately our mental picture of Him kicks in (see chapter 2), and we think, *Been there, done that, bought the T-shirt.* Could it be that we really don't have a clue what God is really like? I contend that we have been told things about God that are not true. He is *not* what we think. If we are not encountering the fulfillment of every one of our desires by our experience with God, we still don't see Him for who He really is. He's beautiful—if we could just see Him. If our minds, hearts, and eyes could be opened for just a moment, there would be a strange resonance inside each of our aching hearts, saying, "This is it. This is what I have always been seeking. This is the reason I was made."

We need to ask ourselves, "How can my internal picture of God be corrected?" It is to answer this question that we now focus our attention. The answer, although quite simple, is profound. There is a doorway through which we will find ourselves surrounded by amazing love, extravagant grace, and intimate friendship. This doorway is the greatest revelation ever to grace our planet. It is the revelation of God's character, made not by someone else, but by Himself through the transparent veil of humanity. God Himself, while on this planet, once said, "I am the door" (John 10:9). We are about to step through this portal of realization and amazement. Prepare your heart to fall into the embrace of perfect love.

---

[1] A psalm of David when he was in the wilderness of Judah. "O God, You are my God; I shall seek You earnestly; my soul thirsts for You, my flesh yearns for You, in a dry and weary land where there is no water" (Ps. 63:1).

[2] "For the heart of this people has become dull, with their ears they scarcely hear, and they have closed their eyes, otherwise they would see with their eyes, hear with their ears, and understand with their heart and return, and I would heal them" (Matt. 13:15).

[3] "For forty years I loathed that generation, and said they are a people who err in their heart, and they do not know My ways" (Ps. 95:10).

[4] "Jesus answered, 'The foremost is, "Hear, O Israel! The Lord our God is one Lord"'" (Mark 12:29).

[5] "Go therefore and make disciples of all the nations, baptizing them in the name of the Father and the Son and the Holy Spirit" (Matt. 28:19).

[6] "The grace of the Lord Jesus Christ, and the love of God, and the fellowship of the Holy Spirit, be with you all" (2 Cor. 13:14).

[7] "The one who does not love does not know God, for God is love" (1 John 4:8).

[8] "Love never fails; but if there are gifts of prophecy, they will be done away; if there are tongues, they will cease; if there is knowledge, it will be done away" (1 Cor. 13:8).

[9] "The Real Truth About Money," *Time*, Jan. 17, 2005.

Chapter Four

The Light of Life

"I am the way, and the truth, and the life; no one comes to the Father but through Me."—JESUS (JOHN 14:6).

"Darkness cannot drive out darkness; only light can do that. Hate cannot drive out hate; only love can do that."—MARTIN LUTHER KING, JR.

It was a sunny afternoon, and I was sitting behind my desk when the phone rang. I picked up the receiver to discover a representative from the University of Washington on the other end. She explained that the university would be hosting a "Religious Views of God" symposium and that a group on campus had submitted my name to fill one of the speaking slots. I asked her for the topic, to which she replied simply, "Oh, just come speak to us about God. We have lots of different folk from different religions, and we would like to hear about God from your perspective, as well." I hung up the phone in shock. This was quite an opportunity.

Over the next few months I prepared painstakingly. Finally the weekend came. I walked into the science lecture hall and immediately noticed that two other lectures were scheduled at the same time as mine in lecture rooms on either side of mine. Glancing at the titles, I saw that the lecture on my left was by a doctor covering the topic "Atheism in the Modern Age," and the one on my right was by another doctor discussing "The Science of Evolution." Curious how they had titled my meeting, I walked to the center lecture room were I was scheduled to speak, and there on the door was a sheet of paper saying simply: "Herb Montgomery—God." (I took it home and have been trying to convince my kids ever since.)

Students began filing in, and as I listened to their conversations, it dawned on me that many of the students whom I was about to address did not view the Bible the same way I do. Basing everything I was planning to say about God on Bible verse after Bible verse, I had committed the cardinal sin of public speaking. I had not fully considered my audience.

Realizing my mistake, I quickly scrapped my notes and began to nervously pray. "God, what am I going to say? I have no time to prepare! This is it, and I have nothing!" I began to sweat in places I didn't even know I had. My knees were having fellowship dinner with one another. The time to begin came, and I still didn't know what to say. Feeling that all was lost, I decided to come clean. But as I was about to confess my utter mistake in preparation, God placed another idea in my head. I decided simply to acquiesce. And God took over.

"I'll give it to you," I said. "Let's say that most of you are right and that there really isn't a God out there. But," I added quickly, "imagine with me that we have been selected and brought together today as the cream of the crop of our planet's intellectually gifted for a very distinct purpose. Some have voted and decided it would be a good idea for there to be a God who is ruling the universe, so we have been given the task of creating a God who will be anything we create Him or Her to be." (I at least had the audience's attention.) Then I asked them, "If you were to create a God to rule the universe, including this planet, what would you *want* God to be like?"

I set the rules, one-word descriptions only, and off we went. Their words began slowly, but the pace quickly escalated to rapid-fire succession. I was writing as fast as I could on the whiteboard at the front of the lecture hall, and within 30 minutes we had the entire board filled—with precious little white space remaining.

Then, as I pondered the words that were on the board, God did a miraculous thing. He tells us, "Do not worry beforehand about what you are to say, but say whatever is given you in that hour; for it is not you who speak, but it is the Holy Spirit" (Mark 13:11).

He certainly did. As I looked at each of those words, God began to bring Bible verses to my memory that communicated the same thought behind each word. And do you know what the most fulfilling 60 minutes of my preaching ministry has been so far? That's right, those next 60 minutes. I had the privilege of spending the next hour taking each description and then going from text to text as I shared with the students that the type of God their hearts really desired was the exact person the Bible paints God to be. "This may not be what some church has taught you. This may not be what some Christian has shown you. But the God that you desire in your heart of hearts, the God that you want in your inmost soul, is the God *the Bible* offers you."

The students were dead silent as they listened in rapt attention.

After the lecture, two young people came forward. One of them asked, "Is there a church anywhere that teaches what you have shared this afternoon?" I assured them there was but that they were a little different. He said, "That's OK; we're different, and what you've said today is different." A few months later they were baptized.

What has always challenged me is that these students' hearts knew "instinctively" what a good God should be like. And they were shocked to discover that, in contrast to what modern Christianity says, the Bible actually offers a God that is truly just what they had wanted Him to be like.

This shouldn't come as such a surprise. After all, the God who fashioned their hearts[1] also supernaturally and continuously keeps alive a hunger and longing for the unseen, the spiritual, the love that comprises eternity.[2] God does this in hope that we might "feel" after Him and "find" Him.[3] Paul tells us that the knowledge of God has been supernaturally preserved in us "instinctively."[4]

This is why there is such a thing called atheism. For 1,700 years, out of the ashes of Dark Ages Christianity, a picture of God emerged that was so out of harmony with what we know to be good, beautiful, and attractive that finally honest souls emotionally and intellectually rebelled. This picture of God was so out of harmony with the "instinctive" knowledge of what a divine being should be like that many simply concluded that if God is like that, He can't exist. Although we don't agree with atheism's conclusion, how it got there strikes a resonant chord with all of us. The next time someone tells you they don't believe in God, ask them to describe this God in which they don't believe. You'll be shocked to discover that you don't believe in that God either.

While on earth Jesus stated that He is the "way" to God, the "truth" about God, and the "life" of God incarnate (John 14:6). What do you think Jesus was seeking to communicate through these weighty words?

As we have seen in these four chapters, humanity's fundamental dilemma is a deeply grounded misconception of the character of the God of this universe. Yet, in the midst of Satan's multitudinous attempts to distort God's character, God Himself took on the disguise of humanity and came and lived among us, in an attempt to invade our darkened understandings and to leave behind the crystal-clear presentation of who and what He really is.

Again and again the Bible uses the contrasting imagery of darkness and light. And if you were to ask most people what the darkness symbolized, they would tell you flat out: "Sin." But I am going to ask you to go a little deeper with me into what the Bible is really trying to communicate. Jesus said, "I am the Light of the world."[5] Jesus was the crystal-clear revelation of what type of being God really is. Jesus shed the light of the knowledge of God's character upon our hearts.[6] The light here is the truth concerning the character of God. The darkness, being the opposite of light, would be all of the lies that darken our hearts in relation to His love. Sin is simply the result, or fruit, of the darkness, not the darkness itself. If you were to turn off the lights, it would become increasingly harder to see. This inability to see God is truly the result of the dark lies that prevail in our world today.

What we are after is to have this darkness dispelled on a personal heart level in each of us. This is our goal. We are in search of encountering God's character. We are on a journey that we hope will bring us to a life-changing encounter with His thoughts and feelings toward us. God lived among us in the person of Jesus of Nazareth, in hopes that we would see past His actions to His heart behind those actions and then realize—this is God! This is the type of person God really is!

My hope is that the light of Jesus will illuminate your darkened understanding right now. I pray that through this book the dawning of the truth about God will begin to arise and dispel the lies that all of us have had in our hearts concerning what God is really like. Paul, Christianity's premier missionary evangelist and author of much of the New Testament, longed for others to come to a true knowledge of God for themselves. Notice his words to Christians living in the town of Corinth: "For God, who said, 'Light shall shine out of darkness,' is the One who has shone in our hearts to give the Light of the knowledge of the glory of God in the face of Christ" (2 Cor. 4:6).

I want to break this text down. It was through the "word" of God that He once brought light out of darkness in the creation of this planet.[7] Today we find darkness in our hearts. This darkness is not physical but perceptual. Notice that this darkness is more than an intellectual darkness; it affects us emotionally. Paul did not say that God is shining into our minds. The lies are held much deeper. The lies reside in our hearts, and it is here that God is seeking to be understood. Remember, it is the heart from which our experience in life flows.[8] It is on a heart level that genuine faith takes place.[9] It is not an intellectual belief that changes us but a belief that takes place in our hearts.[10] This is where God is shining! Yet notice the *means* through which He is seeking to dispel the darkness in our hearts. It is the face of Jesus.

Have you seen His face? This should be the desire and goal for each of us. Never has a person looked into His face and remained the same. For it is in Jesus' face that we encounter the truth about the One who is love.

It was a change in how Adam and Eve "saw"[11] that caused the change from loving fidelity to self-centered self-preservation. My hope is that we will experience, in the light of Jesus' face, a change in the way we "see." In having the truth about God restored to us, may we be changed from a religious experience rooted in self-centered self-preservation to loving, other-centered fidelity.

Paul wrote to the Romans that humanity once "knew God" but that our "hearts were darkened."[12] David, ancient king of the Israelites, revealed that the root of Israel's constant rebellion was that they did not "know" God.[13] Jesus came as a member of the triune God incarnate with the intent of revealing the truth about God's character. Through this revelation He would remove our misapprehension of God's thoughts and feelings, and restore us to the love for which we were made. Jesus came to "destroy the works of the devil" (1 John 3:8). These works are an endless round of subtle deceptions concerning the character of God. It was because we had fallen prey to these lies that the "only begotten God" came to "explain" to us what God is really like.[14]

Jesus, throughout His entire life on this earth, spoke to us through His words and through His actions. He came for the purpose of presenting to us the characteristics and qualities of God. In the New Testament book of Luke, Jesus said that His purpose was to declare to us the "kingdom of God."[15] What did He mean by "kingdom of God"? He had told Nicodemus, a respected church leader of the day, that unless he were born again, he couldn't even "see" it.[16]

Mark records Jesus as asking, "How shall we picture the kingdom of God, or by what parable shall we present it?" When Jesus said, "The kingdom of heaven is like . . . ," He was not talking about the dimensions of mansions or composition of streets, but rather explaining to us the Person who governs there. It was deception over the character of this Person that led us into the captivity of sin, and Jesus knew that it was the truth and only the truth that had the power to make us free.

---

[1] "He who fashions the hearts of them all" (Ps. 33:15).

[2] "He has planted eternity in the human heart" (Eccl. 3:11, NLT).

[3] "That they should seek God, in the hope that they might feel after him and find him. Yet he is not far from each one of us" (Acts 17:27, RSV).

[4] "For the truth about God is known to them instinctively. God has put this knowledge in their hearts" (Rom. 1:19, TLB).

[5] "Then Jesus again spoke to them, saying, 'I am the Light of the world; he who follows Me will not walk in the darkness, but will have the Light of life'" (John 8:12).

[6] "For God, who said, 'Light shall shine out of darkness,' is the One who has shone in our hearts to give the Light of the knowledge of the glory of God in the face of Christ" (2 Cor. 4:6).

[7] "Then God said, 'Let there be light;' and there was light" (Gen 1:3).

[8] "Watch over your heart with all diligence, for from it flow the springs of life" (Prov. 4:23).

[9] "For with the heart a person believes, resulting in righteousness, and with the mouth he confesses, resulting in salvation" (Rom. 10:10).

[10] "And Philip said, 'If you believe with all your heart, you may.' And he answered and said, 'I believe that Jesus Christ is the Son of God'" (Acts 8:37). "And He said to them, 'O foolish men and slow of heart to believe in all that the prophets have spoken!'" (Luke 24:25). See the introduction to this book for a further explanation of these texts.

[11] "When the woman *saw* that the tree was good for food, and that it was a delight to the eyes, and that the tree was desirable to make one wise, she took from its fruit and ate; and she gave also to her husband with her, and he ate. Then the eyes of both of them were opened, and they knew that they were naked; and they sewed fig leaves together and made themselves loin coverings" (Gen. 3:6, 7).

[12] "For even though they knew God, they did not honor Him as God or give thanks, but they became futile in their speculations, and their foolish heart was darkened" (Rom. 1:21).

[13] "For forty years I loathed that generation, and said they are a people who err in their heart, and they do not know My ways" (Ps. 95:10).

[14] "No one has seen God at any time; the only begotten God who is in the bosom of the Father, He has explained Him" (John 1:18).

[15] "But He said to them, 'I must preach the kingdom of God to the other cities also, for I was sent for this purpose'" (Luke 4:43).

[16] "Jesus answered and said to him, 'Truly, truly, I say to you, unless one is born again he cannot see the kingdom of God'" (John 3:3).

Chapter Five

What Is Truth?

"The root word of truth is the same as betrothal. Truth is, therefore, more than mere intellectual facts that convince the mind, but rather that which binds the heart in betrothal to God."—JONATHAN OTTO.

"No lie can live forever."—MARTIN LUTHER KING, JR.

Christians today use the word "truth" a lot. We say we are going to go and share *the truth* with someone, and normally we are talking about some intellectually doctrinal fact, or worse, some lifestyle standard regarding such issues as same-sex marriages, abortion, modern evolutionary science, or prayer in public school. As amazing or beneficial as these doctrinal facts may be, or as important as we feel a lifestyle standard is, Jesus said that the truth is much greater. When He used the word "truth," He was not referring to the religious issues of His day or to the doctrinal controversies of His culture. Rather, He was defining truth as the true picture of the Father. Many of us underestimate the meaning of truth. The truth that Jesus was endeavoring to illuminate for us was not simply Bible facts to which we mentally assent or to which even demons and the devil would assent. Rather, Jesus was seeking to share with us *the truth*, which would surpass mental stimuli alone and touch us at a deep heart level.

I would like you to get in touch with your emotions for just a moment. I am going to make a statement, and I would like you to pay close attention to what emotions this statement evokes deep within your heart. Are you ready? Let your heart feel . . .

"1 + 1 = 2"

What? You aren't feeling anything? You aren't feeling that wellspring of emotions that makes you want to go proclaim it to the world? Well, of course you're not! (Unless maybe you're an elementary math teacher.) The reason is simple: this statement doesn't stimulate your heart at all because it is simply the reiteration of a fact. And no matter how incredible or amazing facts may be, they typically stimulate only the intellect. Too many times we have been convinced but not converted. Facts may change our mind about something, but the truth that Jesus came to give us changes our hearts. What is it that changes us at such a heart level? Love! Love is the truth of what God is really like.

Think back to a time you were in love. What words would you use to describe it? If you say, "It was an intellectually stimulating experience," would that be a fair summary of what you had experienced? This makes us laugh, because love produces more than intellectual stimuli; love moves us at a much deeper level—the heart level. It is at this heart level that God is seeking to move us. What is it that moves us at this deep heart level? Again, it's love.

Does this mean that doctrinal facts are irrelevant? By no means! But in order for doctrinal facts to become *the truth*, they must reveal the One who is the truth: God, with His extravagant love for us. This love moves our hearts, along with our intellects.

Jesus not only sought to share with us the truth of God's love through His stories; He also sought to exemplify God's true character before our very eyes, leaving us a living, breathing demonstration of what God is really like. To Philip He said, "He who has seen me has seen the Father" (John 14:9). Yet we really didn't catch it. In the midst of seeking to reveal the truth about God, Jesus was compelled to cry, "The heart of this people has become dull, with their ears they scarcely hear, and they have closed their eyes, otherwise they would see with their eyes, hear with their ears, and understand with their heart and return, and I would heal them" (Matt. 13:15).

Two things are painfully obvious in this statement. First, Jesus was seeking to communicate something that was not to be understood merely on an intellectual level. It was something He desired us to understand with our hearts. It is alarming that to many modern Christians the statement "God loves you" stimulates precious little more than the statement "1 + 1 = 2." We have turned the "truth" into an intellectual fact to which we mentally assent but rarely encounter with our hearts.

Second, Jesus wanted us to know that "understanding with our hearts" would bring "healing" to us. The prophet Malachi foretold that the "Sun" would one day rise, and that there would be "healing in his rays."[1] We understand this to be a prophecy of Jesus, who is the Sun of righteousness. But why does Malachi liken Jesus' coming to the dawn? Why does he call Jesus the "Sun"?

What is the darkness? Lies. What is the light? It is the truth about God's love. Have you ever watched a sunrise? I grew up in West Virginia and can remember being up in the morning watching those first beams of light cresting over the mountains, dispelling the darkness of the night and introducing a brand-new day.

Could it be that Jesus' coming was to be just as that sunrise? Could it have been likened to a sunrise on earth's darkened misunderstandings of God? The incarnation of Jesus was to shine forth in a day dawning brilliance, illuminating us with the true picture of God so that these rays of truth would dispel our darkened misconceptions and misunderstandings. His coming would scatter the darkness in our hearts concerning our understanding of the character of God and usher in, in a historical sense, a *new day* and with it healing. Look at the language the Gospel writers used to describe the coming of Jesus.

"Because of the tender mercy of our God, with which the Sunrise from on high will visit us, *to shine upon those who sit in darkness and the shadow of death*, to guide our feet into the way of peace" (Luke 1:78, 79).

"Now when Jesus heard that John had been taken into custody, He withdrew into Galilee; and leaving Nazareth, He came and settled in Capernaum, which is by the sea, in the region of Zebulun and Naphtali. This was to fulfill what was spoken through Isaiah the prophet: 'The land of Zebulun and the land of Naphtali, by the way of the sea, beyond the Jordan, Galilee of the Gentiles—the people who were sitting in darkness saw a great light, and those who were sitting in the land and shadow of death, upon them a light dawned'" (Matt. 4:12-16).

The apostle John put it this way: "In Him was life, and the life was the Light of men. The Light shines in the darkness. . . . There was the true Light which, coming into the world, enlightens every man" (John 1:4-9). "And the Word became flesh, and dwelt among us, and we saw His glory [love]" (verse 14). It is this same glory which Moses asked to see.[2] God responded by causing all His "goodness" to pass before Moses. God's glory is His character, His goodness. If you were to sum up all of God in one word, the Bible says that word is "love." To see the glory of God is to be overwhelmed with an understanding of the great love that comprises His being. His love is His glory. When John said that the Word (God) became flesh (a human) and dwelt with us, John also adds the result of this encounter. We beheld His "glory"—His love! Above every other truth that individuals can come to know from the Scriptures, the truth that God is love and that He loves them is paramount above all else. Many have mentally assented to this as a fact, but precious few have encountered the meaning and beauty of the truth of God's love for themselves. The majority of us are still in need of having God explained to us. We have questions, misunderstandings, and misgivings. It was in answer to all of these that God Himself came and, in self-revelation, gave Himself. "No one has seen God at any time; the only begotten *God* who is in the bosom of the Father, He has explained Him" (John 1:18). Jesus is the explanation of God that every human heart longs for, whether it realizes it or not.

Jesus revealed the character of God not only through His life. The greatest revelation of the character of God ever to grace this planet was the revelation Jesus made of God in His death. When Jesus was born, the prophet Simeon said of Him, "This Child is appointed for the fall and rise of many in Israel, and for a sign to be opposed—and a sword will pierce even your own soul—to the end that thoughts from many hearts may be revealed" (Luke 2:34, 35). The cross would be the event that would unveil what was in our hearts and in Satan's heart, but most important, it would reveal the heart of God.

A person's character is revealed through that person's actions.[3] And "character" means the innermost thoughts and feelings. Through a person's actions a person's heart is revealed. When we apply this to our understanding of the purpose of the cross, Simeon's words take on new meaning. Could it be that God's primary purpose through Calvary was to reveal what His heart really is toward us? John recorded Jesus' own testimony concerning the purpose of the cross. Jesus said, "Now My soul has become troubled; and what shall I say, 'Father, save Me from this hour'? But for this purpose I came to this hour" (John 12:27). The hour mentioned here is the time of the cross, and Jesus was about to reveal its purpose. "Father, glorify Your name" (verse 28). Did you catch that? The purpose of Calvary, according to Jesus, was that the name of God be glorified! But what does that mean?

Names are important in the Bible. Children were named on the eighth day of their life because names were indicative of a person's character and the parents were waiting to see that character revealed.

In the Old Testament there was a man named Nabal who spoke abusively to King David's servants. In her plea to David to spare her husband and their servants, his wife, Abigail, informed him that as Nabal's name was, so was he.[4] Nabal means "fool." She was pleading her case with David and his men on the basis that Nabal was just what his name implied—a fool. (Aren't you gland your parents didn't name you Nabal?)

Jacob is another example. The name Jacob, meaning supplanter, was given to him after it was witnessed that he, at birth, was trying to supplant Esau's position as the firstborn.[5] Can you imagine being named according to your character or personality? I am so glad I was born in the twentieth century. Biblical names revealed people's characters, and Jesus used this cultural understanding to describe the purpose of Him going to the cross! He said that He had been divinely brought to the hour of Calvary for the specific purpose of "glorifying," or revealing, the "name" of God.

Does God have a name? What does His name reveal concerning His character? Jesus' primary objective in going to the cross was to reveal to the world the type of person God is, in contrast to the lies with which Satan has tried to deceive us. The Bible records God talking about His name. "Then a voice came out of heaven: 'I have both glorified it [throughout Jesus' life], and will glorify it again [through Jesus' death].' So the crowd of people who stood by and heard it were saying that it had thundered; others were saying, 'An angel has spoken to Him.' Jesus answered and said, 'This voice has not come for My sake, but for your sakes. Now judgment is upon this world; now the ruler of this world will be cast out'" (John 12:28-31).

Now! Now the universe, including this fallen planet, will be able to see the truth concerning the character of God. Now the ruler of this world with all of his lies will be cast out. Notice how Paul shared this with the Colossians: "When He had disarmed the rulers and authorities [the devil and his host], He made a public display of them, having triumphed over them through [the cross]" (Col. 2:15). Jesus, through the revelation of His Father at Calvary, disarmed Satan and his authorities of their lies and made a public display, a spectacle, of them, and triumphed over them. This is it! The cross was the greatest revelation ever given to this planet of what type of being God really is.

Jesus again points us to the primary purpose of Calvary in His prayer for His disciples. "After Jesus said this, He looked toward heaven and prayed: 'Father, the time has come. Glorify your Son, that your Son may glorify you'" (John 17:1, NIV). This was Jesus' main concern, that His Father be clearly portrayed before our eyes. Why? Notice His next statement. "Now this is eternal life: that they may know you, the only true God, and Jesus Christ, whom you have sent" (verse 3, NIV). Remember, God made us for love. We fell from the love for which we were made through lies about the character of God. Jesus is seeking to restore us to the truth about God so that He can also restore us through the truth to the love for which we were originally intended. I would like you to keep in mind the ideas we discussed in the previous chapters as we continue with Jesus' prayer.

"I pray also for those who will believe in me through their message, that all of them [plural] may be one [singular], Father, just as you are in me and I am in you [exactly what exists among the Godhead]. May they [plural] also be in us [singular plurality] so that" "they [plural] may be one [singular], as we are one" (verses 20, 22, NIV). "I in them and You in Me, that they may be perfected in unity, so that the world may know that You sent Me, and loved them, even as You have loved Me" (verse 23).

What an amazing discovery! Could this be what Christianity is all about? Restoring human hearts to the love for which they were made through encountering the truth about God and His love for them? Notice Jesus' closing statement.

"Father, I desire that they also, whom You have given Me, be with Me where I am . . . O righteous Father, although the world has not known You, yet I have known You" (verses 24, 25). "I have made you known to them, and will continue to make you known in order that the love you have for me may be in them and that I myself may be in them" (verse 26, NIV).

Did you catch it? "Father, the world does not know You." This is humanity's fundamental problem. We see God out there, but He is not what the masses have understood or portrayed Him to be. God is not, I believe, what any of us have thought Him to be. We don't know Him. And it is this darkness, just like the darkness between my dad and me, that keeps our hearts at bay, never truly being able to engage in the love for which God made us. It is this darkness—these lies—that Jesus came to expose. Why? "In order that the love you have for me may be in them." In order that the love that passes between members of the Godhead may be in us, flowing horizontally between us and each other as human beings and vertically between us and God. The veil is beginning to be lifted. Both purpose and means have been revealed. God's heart cry is to restore us to the experience of His love through the revelation and restoration of a knowledge of Himself in our hearts.

FINDING THE FATHER

I would like to close this chapter by sharing the words of God recorded by the prophet Ezekiel during the captivity of the children of Israel in the Babylonian Empire: "'As I passed by again, I saw that the time had come for you to fall in love. I covered your naked body with my coat and promised to love you. Yes, I made a marriage covenant with you, and you became mine.' This is what the Sovereign Lord says" (Eze. 16:8. TEV).

I truly believe that the Lord is looking down on you at this very moment reading this book, inviting you, ever so gently, to *see Him as He really is*, whispering softly in your ear, "It's time for you to fall in love."

"'In that day,' declares the Lord, 'you will call me "my husband"; you will no longer call me "my master."'" (Hosea 2:16, NIV).

Do you want this encounter, dear friend? I want it for you, and you indeed can have it. Regardless of who you are or what you have done, it can be yours if you want it. Follow me through the remainder of this book as we seek to understand the God that Calvary sought to reveal. But before we look to the cross, I want to discuss one of the greatest lies about God and what He is like that exists today.

---

[1] "But for you who fear my name, the Sun of justice will rise with healing in his rays, and you will come out leaping like calves from the stall" (Mal. 3:20, New Jerusalem).

[2] "Then Moses said, 'I pray You, show me Your glory!' And He said, 'I Myself will make all My goodness pass before you, and will proclaim the name of the Lord before you; and I will be gracious to whom I will be gracious, and will show compassion on whom I will show compassion.' But He said, 'You cannot see My face, for no man can see Me and live!'" (Ex. 33:18-20).

[3] "Even a child is known by his actions" (Prov. 20:11, NIV).

[4] "Please do not let my lord pay attention to this worthless man, Nabal, for as his name is, so is he. Nabal is his name and folly is with him; but I your maidservant did not see the young men of my lord whom you sent" (1 Sam. 25:25).

[5] "Afterward his brother came forth with his hand holding on to Esau's heel, so his name was called Jacob; and Isaac was sixty years old when she gave birth to them" (Gen. 25:26).

Chapter Six

If God Loves Me . . .

"It's not the prayers God answers that keep us up late at night."—UNKNOWN.

*"No evil ever came from [God's] hands. . . . Let this truth be fixed in
our hearts . . . whenever we are troubled with the thorn or the thistle, with
poisonous or useless weed, with noxious beast . . . or with any other countless
inconveniences and pains or our present condition; whenever we feel ready to
faint by reason of fighting without and fears within, let us remember that
God made all things good, and avoiding hard thoughts of Him, say,
An enemy hath done this."*—G. H. PEMBER.

Before we continue our quest, I would like to address what I consider
to be the greatest obstacle in people's lives that prevents them from
truly "feeling" as though God loves them. Don't get me wrong, I am
not implying that our belief in God's love for us should be dependent on
whether or not we feel as though He loves us. We should believe that
God loves us regardless of how we feel. Having stated that, let me ask you
something. Have you ever been loved? Truly, if we believe that we are
loved by God there will be some emotional involvement, but many today
have turned God's love for them into an intellectual fact to which they
have mentally assented, and simply left their heart starving outside. God
made us for the pleasure of loving while simultaneously being loved, and
whenever I have experienced love, my heart has been involved at the very
center. This is what God is inviting us to encounter with Him—love. Yet
so many hearts are plagued with the question of "why?" "If God loves me
so much, why did He allow . . . to happen to me?"

I have the privilege of traversing this globe in order to share the
greatest truth that a human being can ever encounter, and that is the fact
that God is love and that God loves you! While this news induces excite-

ment for many, for another group, because of the sick tragedies they have supposedly been divinely "allowed" to experience, the statement that God loves them fills them with anger and sometimes rage.

I can remember presenting a seminar in Michigan. My presentations were finished, and I was walking out the door of the church to my rental car when I saw a woman who looked as if she had been crying. She apologetically asked me if she could speak with me and then proceeded to tell me her story. She had listened with rapt attention all weekend long. She had felt her heart wanting to believe the truths I was sharing concerning God's love for her, but she could not bring her heart to believe. She told me about an experience she had in Sunday school as a small girl. She had asked her teacher one week why Jesus doesn't answer prayer. Now, I am sure this Sunday school teacher was well-meaning, but his answer produced a seed in this little girl's heart that would grow through the years and produce emotional pain in her relationship with God, even into her adult years. This teacher advised her, without finding out what the little girl was praying for, that she just *wasn't being specific enough in her prayers.*

So this little girl went home and began to give Jesus detailed directions to her house. Then, she proceeded to give Him meticulous instructions on how to get from her front door to her bedroom. Next, she began to give God detailed descriptions of what her father and her brothers would be wearing that night as they sexually molested her. This took place, she said, every night of her life until she ran away at age 14. She looked me straight in the eyes and said, "Never once did God ever answer my prayers for Him to intervene and make it stop. If God loves me, why didn't He answer my cries for help?" The tears then began to stream down her cheeks as she sobbed. My heart broke.

Now, don't get me wrong, I know Jesus does answer prayers, but what happens with cases like this one? I was recently conducting presentations for a group of young people when I was met at the door by a 16-year-old girl who asked if she could talk with me. As with the previous scenario, she began very graciously by saying, "I want to believe what you have been telling me of God's love for me, but if God loves me the way that you say He does, why did He *allow* me to be raped?" Her story, which had happened the year before she met me, was horrendously gut-wrenching as well.

At another series of presentations in Canada, a woman got up from the back of the church and headed straight up to the front where I was

standing. Have you ever been slapped? Do you know that look in someone's eyes just before the hand makes contact with your face? Well, she
had that same look in her eye all the way from the back of that church.
Within inches of my face (I know most preachers exaggerate, but this is no
exaggeration) she pointed her finger at me and scolded, "Don't you dare
tell me that God loves me! If God loves me the way you say He does, why
did He allow me to be sexually abused by my father, who was a *minister*?"
Being raised by a single mother who had taught me at a young age when
to open my mouth in response to an angry woman and when to keep it
shut, I simply took one step back and let her vent.

What do you say to people who have suffered gross injustice at the
hands of another person? How do you comfort those who have cried out
to God for help, but no help came, and now they feel as if God has abandoned them?

These questions make us very uncomfortable. And rightly so. God
forbid we should ever be comfortable with stories such as these. However,
one of the greatest reasons I believe these questions make us uncomfortable is that we don't like to talk about God letting us down. We'd rather
have a God who always comes through for us. Yet, there are thousands of
folks who have experienced times in their life when it *appears* that He did
abandon them. When they ask why, we are uncomfortable because we
don't have a good answer.

Have you ever noticed that many times we are busy answering the
questions that nobody is asking, while the questions that people really are
asking make us way too uncomfortable to answer?

The question of "why," in relation to human tragedy and suffering, is one of the most uncomfortable questions there is to tackle. I am
convinced, however, that if we are going to be culturally relevant, while
painting a biblically pure picture of God and His love for us, this question must be addressed. It must receive our attention. No other question
so powerfully keeps people's hearts away from being able to enter into a
meaningful relationship with this God who claims to love them so much.

I believe that God's shoulders are big enough, God is transparent
enough, and God is patient enough to handle any question we could possibly ask Him. God's chest is big enough for us to pound on when we
don't understand. I know that this topic is highly emotionally charged, yet
I would like us to consider it rationally. I want you to know that what I
am about to say is from my own pain as well. You see, my wife and I have

buried two children. I'm not saying that we have suffered more than those who may be reading this book, but I do want you to know that I have suffered too. What I am about to share with you comes out of my own personal wrestling. I'm sharing with you in hopes that the comfort with which I have been comforted may be a source of comfort to you as well.*

---

* "Blessed be the God and Father of our Lord Jesus Christ, the Father of mercies and God of all comfort, who comforts us in all our affliction so that we will be able to comfort those who are in any affliction with the comfort with which we ourselves are comforted by God" (2 Cor. 1:3, 4).

Chapter Seven

The Question of Why

///

"Everything happens for a reason."—UNKNOWN.

"Creator—a comedian whose audience is afraid to laugh."
—H. L. (HENRY LOUIS) MENCKEN.

"Free will is what has made evil possible. Why, then, did God give [creatures] free will? Because free will, though it makes evil possible, is also the only thing that makes possible any love or goodness or joy worth having."—C. S. LEWIS.

"We have to believe in free will. We have no choice."—ISAAC SINGER.

"The happiness God desires for His creatures is . . . ecstasy of love. . . . And for that they must be free."—C. S. LEWIS.

Although God is able to handle the question *why*, the very question is based on unbiblical, yet cultural, assumptions. When we ask *why*, we assume that: (1) if God had *wanted* to prevent something, (2) He *could* have, (3) but since He *didn't*, (4) He must have *wanted* it to happen.

If God is up in heaven meticulously controlling every event that transpires on Planet Earth, allowing some things to happen and preventing other things from happening, it would seem logical to conclude that He is allowing things, even bad things, to happen only because He wants them to happen for some good reason. Therefore, when we ask the question *why*, we are really asking for the *divine reason for why this has been allowed to happen to us if God loves us so much.* From this reasoning, many have concluded that *everything happens for a reason.* Some will say that nothing happens that is not God's will, or rather nothing happens to you for which God did not have a purpose.

Is this really what the Bible teaches? If it is, I don't see how we can escape the conclusion that we serve a God who, on some level and for some reason, approves of child molestation and rape. I cannot accept this. If it is true, we are left looking into the face of a good God wondering how rape, kidnapping, murder, accidents, and molestation fit into His will. His will becomes mysterious, and we are told, "We are just not wise enough to understand yet, but one day He'll show us how this evil was actually a good thing. This evil is actually for a good reason, and one day you'll see." Is this really how it all works?

What we fail to notice in this paradigm of reasoning is that darkness begins to enshroud our heart-level understanding of what type of being God really is and how He feels about us. There are four lies that this type of reasoning ultimately leads us to believe about God. The problem is that most of us haven't realized what we are saying with these false assumptions. The first lie: everything happens for a divine reason. The second: evil happens for a greater good. The third: in evil, God is up to something (most assume that it's something good, so they are willing to put up with tragedy and simply *trust* God that He knows what He is doing). And if we say that God allows only things that are for a higher good to happen, we inadvertently fall into the fourth and most dangerous lie: there is no such thing as evil. We say that it's simply a matter of perspective. We say that if we could see things as God does, we would see that this pain is truly a blessing. We say that these violations are really for our higher good.

I want to repeat, these are all lies. The Bible warns us of this type of reasoning: "Woe to those who call evil good, and good evil; who substitute darkness for light and light for darkness; who substitute bitter for sweet and sweet for bitter!" (Isa. 5:20).

I believe all tragedy can fit into one of three categories: (1) things God can prevent—and does; (2) things God can prevent—but doesn't (for a good reason); and (3) a separate and distinct category which we will be looking at in the following chapters, simply because there are some atrocities that it would be blasphemous to put into these first two categories.

Take the two we are looking at presently—child molestation and rape. Do they fit into either of the first two categories? Not at all! So we desperately need a third category in which to understand why these crimes happen.

To be honest, modern Christianity does not offer us that third category. But the Bible does! I would like to share what the Bible states concerning the four assumptions and the four lies that support the current Christian viewpoint. In the most famous prayer ever prayed there is an alarming statement that runs in blatant contradiction to the above reasoning. It is in the Lord's prayer, and we are taught to pray, "Your will be done, on earth as it is in heaven" (Matt. 6:10).

The cultural assumption is that God's will is always done in our lives. If God wants it to happen, it will, we say. Notice the contrary implication of Jesus' prayer. Where is God's will being done right now? The prayer is clear—in *heaven*. Where are we to pray for God's will to be done? On *earth*. Why pray for God's will to be done on earth if it already naturally is? God's will *is* being done in heaven. Where is God's will not being done, and where are we to intercede and pray for God's will to be done? *On earth*.

The Bible teaches that God is currently engaged in a formidable struggle to have His will done on this planet. In many instances God does not get His way. Often, what God wants is *not* being done.

The Gospel of Luke states that the church leaders and lawyers of Jesus' day actually *rejected* the will of God for their lives.[1] This reveals to us that we are capable of rejecting what God wants, His will. We can act in accordance with our own wills. Not everything is part of His plan. Not everything is going His way. To prove this takes just one word—rape. Is rape ever God's will? It is never God's will for violation of this level of intimate magnitude to take place. This action is unfair, unjust, and evil.

Has God made a world in which His will can be delayed, thwarted, and even prevented from ever happening? Can God's will be prevented from ever happening even throughout the ceaseless ages of eternity? The Bible's answer seems to be yes. Peter, one of Jesus' original disciples, tells us that God's will for everyone who has ever lived is to repent and not perish.[2] Paul stated that God wishes for everyone to be saved and to come to the knowledge of the truth.[3] Yet there are some individuals who are going to prevent His desire for them from ever happening throughout the boundless ages of eternity.

And so we discover from the Bible that there are many things happening that God does not want to happen. There is not a divine reason for everything. Evil activities and events can transpire against the will of God. Therefore, these events are not for a higher good, but are the result of the decisions of some other free moral agent. These events are intended to bring, not good, but harm. There is much evil on this planet behind which

God is not up to anything. His desire is that the evil event would never take place. As Scripture states, not everything on Planet Earth is part of God's plan. This is not to say that God doesn't have a plan for our lives. He does, but not everything that happens to us is part of that plan. There is much that happens to us that He was striving against, and yet it happened anyway. Much has taken place in our lives that God must now overcome in order for His plan to succeed.

We may scratch our head and say to ourselves, "Why would God make such a world in which His creation can thwart His own activity and desires? Why would God make a world with this level of freedom?" Or as some have asked: "Why would God make a world that could say *no* to Him?"[4]

It all comes back to the beginning—our picture of God. If we begin with the assumption that God is a being whose chief attribute is control, then it is puzzling why He would make a world in which He chooses to let others control events. But if we start with the premise that God's chief attribute is *love*, then some things begin to make sense.

Let's say that I scheduled and *controlled* my wife's life down to each and every moment of the day. I determined when she woke up each morning and what she would wear. I dictated that she would make breakfast and decided what she would make. Then I scheduled her morning, afternoon, evening, and night with meticulous detail. Her entire day was scheduled and controlled, including bathroom breaks. Would you say that I was the most loving husband ever to walk the planet? Of course not. You would say that I was a control freak! We look at people who exert that much meticulous control as being emotionally and psychologically unhealthy. And yet we continually attribute this characteristic of meticulously controlling everything to God.

Freedom and control are not synonyms but antonyms. Does God want to control you or give you freedom? It must be one or the other. We can't be free and controlled at the same time.

Now, if we start from the premise that God's chief attribute is not control but *love*, we begin to see a whole different picture. Our three-in-one God created us out of a pleasurable experience of love. Their desire was to share Their love and have others enter into its joy. God, being a God of love, created us for love. Yet for love to be experienced, the objects of that love must be given *freedom*!

This brings us to the most important question we can ask. There are many things happening that God doesn't want to happen, and yet He does not *prevent* them from taking place. Why? Remember, we assume that if God wanted to prevent something, He *could*. After all, God can do anything. But does the Bible teach that there is nothing God can't do? Or does the Bible teach that some things are impossible for even an omnipotent God? The Bible teaches that "with" God all things are possible.[5] It never teaches that all things are possible even when we are in "opposition" to God.

It is vital that we stand on Biblical ground here rather than on culturally acceptable opinions, even if that culture is modern Christianity. Paul wrote, "In hope of eternal life, which God, who cannot lie . . ." (Titus 1:2). Did you catch that? God, who is omnipotent, cannot lie. So there is, according to the Bible, at least one thing that God can't do. Why can't He lie? Because in order to lie He would have to change the *nature* of His character. Let's look at the nature of a few things and ask some hard questions.

Given the nature of a triangle, can God make a *round* triangle? This question is not elementary or foolish. A triangle, by definition, or rather by its very nature, has three sides. How many sides does a circle have? The answer is two (inside and outside). If God were to make a triangle round, in that moment He would change the nature of the object, and it would cease to be a triangle. This discussion is based on the assumption that God doesn't change the definition or the nature of a triangle.

Can God make you love Him? I'm not asking *will* He make you love Him. I'm sure we would all agree that He won't make us love Him. But if He wanted to, *could* He make you love Him? I have asked this question to thousands of audiences around the globe and every time there are mixed responses. About half of the crowd says yes and the other half says no.

Imagine that I could create a computer chip that would *make* an individual love me. All I would have to do is attach the chip behind the person's right ear, and through an adhesive strip on the back the chip would adjust the electromagnetic waves of the person's brain, making him or her love me.

What if I were to place this chip behind my wife's ear? Would she, at that moment, be loving me? Invariably, the audiences I have asked say no. When asked what is loving me, they answer that it is the chip. But is it really the chip? Who programmed the chip? You see, if I programmed the chip, and the chip is forcing the brain waves in an individual to mimic a love response toward me, then ultimately I am loving myself through the altered individual.

In chapter 3 we established that genuine love, in order to be genuine, is always other–centered. It is something that begins with me and always ends in someone or something else. That is love's *nature*. Now, if I am "loving" myself, we are talking about something that begins with me and ends, not with someone else, but with me. It has become self-centered. Thus, its nature is no longer genuine love. Self-respect is similar to love, but since it begins with me and ends with me, I can't call it love. If I do, I've changed the nature of it; it has ceased to be a "triangle."

So we arrive at the conclusion that even an omnipotent God *cannot make* us love Him. It is not because of a lack of ability in God; the impossibility lies in the nature of the object. God can do all things, but God cannot do nonthings.

Now let's return to our four assumptions. Things are taking place that God wishes would not take place. Then why does He not prevent them? We assume that since He isn't preventing them, He must be wanting them to happen.[6] But He doesn't want them to happen! Could it be that it's not because He chooses not to prevent them, but rather because He *can't*?

Let me be clear that nothing limits God, or else He would cease to be God. But in choosing to grant us freedom, God has chosen to limit Himself in what He can and cannot do. If this is what the Bible teaches, then we have discovered the third category: (1) things God can prevent and does; (2) things God could prevent but chooses not to for a good reason; and (3) things God wants to prevent but can't because He has granted freedom.

When talking about child molestation and rape, we must see God's action—or inaction—through a biblical third category that does not slander His character by even hinting that He approves of these evil acts. Any time God can prevent child molestation and rape, He does! And if He doesn't prevent it, it is not because He wants it to happen (even for a good reason), but that a contradiction between control and free will ties His hands.

I remember a person who was very upset that God could claim to be love and not prevent child molestation. I said, "Why stop there? God should prevent all rapes as well."

She said, "Yes!"

"And," I said, "God should prevent all murders and robberies as well!"

She replied, "Yes, yes!"

Then came the stinger. I said, "God should just prevent all sin!"

Then she understood. There is a delicate balance between control and freedom. Everything that transpires on this planet falls somewhere on a sliding scale between absolute freedom and ultimate control. One day God is going to show us why certain events took place in our lives that He could not prevent.

Let me tell you another story that I believe will help get our minds out of our postmodern reactionist way of thinking into a more biblically realistic paradigm. About three years ago I had two friends who were having a birthday around the same time. They were also friends with each other, so I decided to invite them to my home and have a joint birthday party for the two of them. The problem was that they both lived about seven hours away. I still remember the long silence on the other end of the phone. They said, "Uh, Herb, it's our birthday. Why don't you come to our houses to have our parties?"

So in order to induce them to make the trip, I made a deal. "If you come to my house and celebrate your birthday with my family and me," I said, "then I'll take you to the grocery store, and you can choose anything you want for your party and I'll pay for it." They were on my doorstep seven hours later. They liked the fact that this was all on my tab, and the shopping spree began.

Upon arrival at the grocery store, the first stop was the ice–cream coolers. You know, I've never understood why some people always pick their ice cream first. It's going to melt before you even leave the store, but this is what they wanted. One of them opened the fridge and the other picked up a large container of Breyer's natural vanilla ice cream. You know, the kind with only four ingredients, all of which are in English. You can read and recognize all four of them.[7]

When they put the ice cream in the cart, I immediately gave them "the look." You know, that condescending, condemning, "Don't you know how bad ice cream is for you?" look.[8] Have you ever gotten "the look" when eating something unhealthy? Or rather, have you ever given someone else "the look" when he was eating something unhealthy? Returning the ice cream to the freezer, I replaced it with a large container of vanilla-flavored Rice Dream imitation ice cream and gave them "the look" one more time. I guess they thought I was serious, so they didn't say anything.

Next, we went to the bakery section. They picked up one of those "death by chocolate" cakes and placed it in the cart. I gave them "the look" again and quickly replaced it with one of those sugar-free vanilla diabetic cakes, and placed it in the cart. Then, I gave them "the look" again. Now they were getting frustrated, but they still remained silent, thinking that I had some health conviction that I had to impose on them.

Now we were on our way to the chips and soda aisle. They immediately picked out a big three-liter bottle of Mountain Dew and put it in the cart. I guess they were more passionate about their Mountain Dew than their cake and ice cream, because all I got away with this time was simply reaching for the bottle. I hadn't even touched it yet when the more vocal of the two burst out, "Wait a minute! You said we could choose anything we wanted, and since we came into this store, you have not let us have one thing that we picked!"

I have to pause the story here for a quick moment and simply warn all of you. You really don't want to be my friend. Oh, I know you might think you do, but in reality I will use you at the very moment you least expect it to create illustrations for sermons and books. At least I have the decency not to share my friends' names when I share their stories. Now back to the story. (I wanted this illustration very badly.)

I very calmly responded, "Ah, but you didn't pay attention to what it was I actually said. I said you could *choose* anything you wanted. I never said you could *have* what you chose." And immediately, without any pause or thought about how to respond, the statement I was hoping for came naturally. "Well, if we were never free to have what we chose, then we were never genuinely free to choose it in the first place." Bingo! (By the way, I did let them have what they wanted after my experiment with them.)

This friend of mine tapped into an important quality of *genuine* freedom. In order for freedom to be genuine, it also must possess the quality of being *irrevocable*. This is the *nature* of freedom.

Let's say that I give you the freedom to choose option A or B. I want you to choose option A, but I give you the freedom to choose option A or B. I could force you to have option A and prevent you from experiencing option B. But if I did this, would that still leave you free to choose between A or B? Even if you choose B, you are going to experience A. This is not freedom at all! I would have changed the *nature* of it. In order for freedom to be genuine, it must be irrevocable. I must give you the freedom to choose option A or B, and even if I want you to choose A, I can't step in and prevent the outcome of your decision if you choose B. I could not step in without, at that very moment, revoking freedom, and proving that you were never genuinely, irrevocably free from the beginning.

This is God's predicament. He has the power to prevent evil, but it is impossible to prevent all evil and still give the freedom to choose evil. In other words, it is impossible, even for God, to prevent someone from having option B when he or she chooses it, and maintain the irrevocability of the freedom He originally gave for him or her to choose option A or B.

There is a question that rises from this that must be answered. We will seek to answer it in the next chapter.

------

[1] "But the Pharisees and lawyers rejected the will of God for themselves, not having been baptized by him" (Luke 7:30, NKJV).

[2] "The Lord is not slack concerning His promise, as some count slackness, but is long-suffering toward us, not willing that any should perish but that all should come to repentance" (2 Peter 3:9, NKJV).

[3] "This is good and acceptable in the sight of God our Savior, who desires all men to be saved and to come to the knowledge of the truth" (1 Tim. 2:3, 4).

[4] C. S. Lewis, *The Problem of Pain, The Abolition of Man,* and *Mere Christianity.*

[5] "And looking at them Jesus said to them, 'With people this is impossible, but with God all things are possible'" (Matt. 19:26).

[6] There are many things that God does prevent, some of which we know about, and some we may never know about because they never happened. Remember, we not only are looking at the first two categories but are trying to discover a viable, biblical third category as well. What about the rapes and molestations that God doesn't prevent?

[7] Milk, cream, sugar, natural flavor.

[8] Let me quickly explain for all our health-conscious readers: I'm not poking fun at being healthful, but rather at how we condemn our friends for doing things that are unhealthy.

Chapter Eight

Does the End Justify the Means?

"The end may justify the means as long as there is something that justifies the end."—LEON TROTSKY.

*"No matter what God's power may be,
the first aspect of God is never that of the absolute Master, the Almighty.
It is that of the God who puts Himself on our human level
and limits Himself."*—JACQUES ELLUL.

*"No theodicy that does not take the Devil fully into Consideration
is likely to be persuasive."*—JEFFREY B. RUSSELL.

*"If we are to take the biblical understanding seriously at all, intercession" "changes
the world and . . . it changes what is possible to God."*—WALTER WINK.

Doesn't God sometimes intervene and prevent evil? Yes, and we can safely say, knowing His character, that any time He can intervene He will. But why can He sometimes intervene and not other times? We will probably never completely know this side of eternity. When God shows us one day what was happening behind the scenes of our lives, He will be showing us what tied His hands, what prevented His will from being done at the time. He will not be showing us how a certain rape or molestation was actually something good from His vantage point, something we simply could not see from His point of view. Rather, He will show us where free choices intersected and kept Him at bay when He longed and tried to intervene. In the brokenness of His own heart, He will explain that He was not able to interfere with the irrevocability of a certain circumstance created by the decisions of free moral agents. God created us for love, and love requires genuine freedom. For that freedom to be genuine it must be irrevocable, meaning that people remain free even if they choose something other than what God wants. As difficult and painful as this may be to accept, there are some tragedies that God simply can't prevent. Why? Because even He cannot grant freedom and sit in a position of control at the same time.

"No, no, *no!*" some will say. "The reason God allows some things to happen is that He knows the good that will come out of them." Understand that God allows freedom. We are choosing what is done with that freedom. If God is in complete control and He is allowing circumstances for their ultimate good, then we would be forced to say that for God, the end justifies the means. I don't believe any would agree with that. The end never justifies the means.

Some will say that if we could just see things the way God does, we would thank Him. One day, they say, we will see these awful events from His perspective, not as evils but as blessings. Again, Scripture has strong words for those who would desecrate God's character with such reasoning.

"Woe to those who call evil good, and good evil; who substitute darkness for light and light for darkness; who substitute bitter for sweet and sweet for bitter!" (Isa. 5:20).

Is God meticulously in control of everything happening here, or has He granted freedom? If the nature of this world is one in which everything, even the tragedies, transpires under God's control and happens exactly as He desires for some higher good, what assurance do we have that heaven will be any different from life on this planet? What hope do we have that the pain and suffering will end with the close of this age? What if God should deem some tragic event or suffering to be worthy of affecting us for some higher good in the age to come? What assurance do we have that this nightmare will not happen again? If rape and molestation can sometimes be a good thing, and heaven will be filled with good things, will these atrocities ever end? If this is the type of world that exists when God is in control, then heaven could be a pretty scary place. The chaos of this world proves that God is not in complete control but has granted freedom.

If we compare the "end justifying the means" picture of suffering with the life of Christ, we begin to see that Jesus never used this type of reasoning. A careful look at every event of His life on earth shows that Jesus viewed suffering and tragedy as an alien element, an enemy to be overcome. It was never part of God's plan, but rather something from which He worked to set people free.

I believe this passage from the physician Luke reveals what God's true desires are in relation to human suffering: "You know of Jesus of Nazareth, how God anointed Him with the Holy Spirit and with power, and how He went about doing good and healing all who were oppressed by the devil, for God was with Him" (Acts 10:38).

There is one word that is particularly interesting here—"all." Jesus would walk into villages, and when He departed there was not one ounce of human suffering left. His life was truly an act of invasion. He would enter the scene and bring deliverance to any and all whom His path happened to cross, whom Satan had kept bound.[1] It's also interesting that Jesus never looked for some higher reason for the suffering He encountered. He simply viewed all suffering as an attack from the enemy and immediately set about to accomplish His work of deliverance.

Thus, Jesus healed all with whom He came in contact. There is only one incident where this principle finds an exception, and this was in His hometown of Nazareth. Jesus did not heal there, but not because He saw it as the Father's will that this town should continue experiencing suffering and tragedy. On the contrary, Jesus did not heal there because He *could* not heal there. What was it that prevented Him from being able to bring relief and deliverance? Matthew clearly tells us: "He did not do many miracles there *because of their unbelief*" (Matt. 13:58). Jesus *could* not do many miracles there, and it seems that the mention of this event is to state quite clearly that this was not what God had intended for this town. Once again, we find a situation in which God's desire was thwarted or prevented by the free moral agency of others.

We need to be quite sure of this one key principle if we are to understand why, from our perspective, it may seem that God's answers to prayers or intervention in tragedies may seem so arbitrary. First, Jesus is the exact image or representation of God. If we want to know God's desires or will in regard to our suffering, we can find clear answers in the life of Christ. Jesus made strong statements giving us assurance that He and God are exactly alike. If it doesn't show up in the life of Jesus, then it doesn't exist in the character of God. Notice the following statements by Jesus Himself:

"He who has seen Me has seen the Father" (John 14.9).

"It is the Father, living in me, who is doing his work" (Verse 10, NIV).

"The Son can do nothing of Himself, unless it is something He sees the Father doing; for whatever the Father does, these things the Son also does in like manner" (John 5:19).

The author of Hebrews stated that Jesus was the "exact representation" of the Father.[2]

John put it this way: "No one has seen God at any time; the only begotten God who is in the bosom of the Father, He has explained Him" (John 1:18).

The will of God toward human suffering is revealed in the way Jesus related to it. I believe it is never God's desire for His children to suffer. Jesus' example calls us to believe that suffering is always an enemy element from which God is seeking to save us. Much of today's suffering is being touted as an agency of God to teach us higher lessons, and although I do not disagree that sometimes, and I repeat, *sometimes*, God uses suffering to teach lessons, I believe from the life of Jesus that the suffering and tragedies that continuously surge through this planet are, to a large degree, the work of an enemy in opposition to what God is trying to accomplish. These events are not the workings of God; "an enemy has done this" (Matt. 13:28).

All of this leads me to my point. I believe that any time God can intervene, prevent, or heal, the life of Jesus reveals that *He will*. I also believe that when God does not intervene, prevent, or heal, it is not because He chooses not to, but rather because, in this particular situation, the principle of *genuine human freedom* is preventing Him from accomplishing the deliverance He desires to do as quickly as He desires to do it.

We see this principle in the life of Daniel the prophet as well. Daniel had been fasting and praying for three entire weeks in an effort to receive wisdom and understanding. For 21 days Daniel had petitioned the Almighty to answer his prayer. I want you to stop for a moment and put yourself in Daniel's sandals about day 18. What would be going through your mind? For many, one of two major conclusions would have been made. One: *Well, I guess my prayer is not according to God's will.* They would succumb to a humble resignation that "God knows best" and then stop praying. Many others would think, *Maybe I am too sinful for God to answer my prayer,* and simply give up praying based on their moral deficiencies.

Notice that Daniel did not think like this at all, but persevered in prayer. When God's angel finally showed up to answer his prayer, he explained why it took him 21 days to show up: "Then he said to me, 'Do not be afraid, Daniel, for *from the first day* that you set your heart on understanding this and on humbling yourself before your God, your words were heard, and I have come in response to your words. *But the prince of the kingdom of Persia was withstanding me for twenty-one days*; then behold, Michael, one of the chief princes, came to help me, *for I had been left there with the kings of Persia*. Now I have come to give you an understanding of what will happen to your people in the latter days, for the vision pertains to the days yet future" (Dan. 10:12-14).

The angel states that Daniel's prayer was answered by God the very first day Daniel began praying. The angel Gabriel was sent to bring the answer to Daniel, but something happened in the interim. Gabriel, upon arrival to this planet, was met by the prince of the kingdom of Persia, and was resisted for 21 days. This is hard to believe for us Westerners, who are accustomed to think only of the world we can see. But Scripture seems to be quite clear that there is an in-between world as well, a world in between God's realm in heaven and what we can see here on earth. Up to this point we have considered only the impact that human freedom has on God's ability to carry out His will unhindered. Now the Scriptures are pulling back the veil and showing us that humans are not the only free moral agents in the universe that sometimes get in the way of what God wants to happen.

Now let's back up a bit. What do you think would have happened if Daniel had thought of prayer the way many people view it today? What if Daniel had given up, thinking that his request must be contrary to God's will or that his own moral condition made him unworthy of receiving an answer? It was only Daniel's free moral agent perseverance in prayer that gave Gabriel and Michael the legal right to enter into the dominion of a foreign territory. If Daniel had given up on day 20, this is what I imagine—and this is strictly imagination—would have happened. The prince of the territory of Persia would have responded to both Gabriel and Michael, "Well, Daniel doesn't want you anymore. Go home!" But Daniel did persevere, and Gabriel finally arrived. The point of this whole story vividly illustrates that God's will and our worthiness are not the only parts to the equation of answering prayer. No matter how much we pray, prayer never gives God or angels the right to abuse the free will of others, human or angelic, fallen though they may be.

The natural question arises: "If this is truly how it works, why pray?" This question reveals a misconception in how most of us view prayer. Prayer does not transform God into a vending machine. Prayer is a dynamic reality that gives God greater control and right to intervene than He previously would have had, had a request not been made.

DOES THE END JUSTIFY THE MEANS?

Let me illustrate it this way. You can live a healthy life. You can exercise, eat right, refrain from harmful substances, and still get cancer or some other debilitating disease. Does this mean we shouldn't bother living healthy lives? Absolutely not! Living healthfully gives us an advantage against contracting or developing debilitating illnesses in the future. It does not guarantee that nothing bad will happen, but it does give us an *advantage*.

The same is true of prayer. God does not promise us that we will get everything for which we pray. There are more variables in the equation of answering prayer than just God's will and our willingness. I can pray for the salvation of a brother-in-law all my days, and yet if that friend and relative resists or refuses, my praying does not give God the right to override his free will. Genuine irrevocable freedom is a major variable in how things are transpiring here on Planet Earth. This is why God asks us to place our will alongside His. He asks us to pray that *His* will be done on earth as it is in heaven. Prayer does not guarantee that everything we pray for will happen, but it does give God and us an advantage. God has given this earth to the children of men.[3] This is our home, and just as we can decide who comes into our personal homes and who doesn't, so we can decide who comes into our planetary home.

The problem arises when you realize how many people own this world. Each one of us has the right to let God in or force Him out, and to let Satan in or force him out. When tragedy strikes, we gather as many people as possible to pray, not to more strongly persuade God to act, but, like a democracy, to get as many "votes" for our preferred outcome. We can exercise our freedom to bring God, along with His healing and relief, into the situation.

Yet some will still say, "All things happen according to God's will, but His will is too complex to understand! One day we will understand, but not now."

God's will is not complex. It is the *nature* of a free world that is complex. The delicate balance between control and freedom, when you have millions of free moral decisions happening at any moment, is complex. Yes, one day God will pull back the veil and show us why something happened to us, but rather than showing us why He allowed it or what higher good it accomplished, He will be showing us *how* freedom, with choice, prevented His will from being done in our particular situation. He will show us how His hands were tied, and what it was that tied them.

FINDING THE FATHER

The Bible is clear that God's will is not some mysterious, hard-to-understand concept, where some people are blessed and others suffer. It paints God's will as being quite simple. His plan for all is "good things,"[4] that we would experience "health" and "prosperity."[5] God desires our "welfare" and for us to avoid "calamity."[6] Jesus' life shows us that God's will is to heal us all, to stop all suffering, to intervene in all of life's tragedies, to deliver us *from* evil!

James, in his New Testament book filled with practical pointers for living a Christian life, tells us clearly what is from God and what is not: "Every good thing" is "from above." Then he adds, "from the Father . . . , with whom there is no variation or shifting shadow." If something transpires in our lives that is "good," then we can be assured that is from our heavenly Father. We can be assured that the evil events are *not* from God. Why? Because in the Father there is no variation, no change in character, no transition from kind and loving to sinister. In God there is no "shifting shadow."

Have you ever watched the shadow of an object change or "shift" as the day wears on? The shadow shifts because the position of the sun to the object is constantly changing. James seems to be sharing with us that, in relation to God and us, on God's part there is no shifting shadow. His thoughts and feelings toward us do not change. His position toward us remains constant.

God does only good, and He does not orchestrate evil for good. If this were the case, then every human being would be right in saying, "The end justifies the means."

Notice these words of Jesus' disciple John: "Beloved, I pray that in all respects you may prosper and be in good health, just as your soul prospers" (3 John 2). John is giving us a window into the wishes of the God he serves. God's desire is that we would live prosperous lives and enjoy good health. Some have emphasized here that God desires for us to prosper spiritually, but not always temporally. But this text states that God desires us to prosper just as our soul prospers, implying that the abundant life is more than just spiritual prosperity. God wants us to prosper in every area of our life. Very few things are more frustrating than when an individual makes poor financial decisions and then blames God by saying, "Well, it must not be God's will for me to have money." This tendency is not reserved for our finances only. Many times our unwise decisions set in motion events that prevent us from experiencing the free and joyous life for which we were intended, and then we blame God by stating that these circumstances "must be God's plan." It's not God's doing but our own!

God desires all of us to prosper and be in excellent health. The problem is that God has an enemy who is seeking to "steal and kill and destroy."[7] The abundant life that God intended for us and that Jesus died to give back to us is not a life of suffering. The suffering that many Christians experience is not by God's desire or design. We have an enemy whose primary purpose is to thwart God's plan for our lives by inflicting as much suffering as possible on the objects of God's affection. Notice how the Old Testament prophet Jeremiah illustrates God's desires for us.

"'For I know the plans that I have for you,' declares the Lord 'plans for welfare and not for calamity, to give you a future and a hope'" (Jer. 29:11).

God does not desire for us to experience calamity, but seeks only our welfare. Welfare is defined as the physical, social, and financial conditions under which somebody may live satisfactorily. God's desire for all of us is that we would have all our needs met, and then find our truest fulfillment for all our desires in Him and His love for us. This is the reason we were made; this is the life God chose for each of us from before our birth. Yet as we have already discussed, we and God are not the only variables in the equation. There are other wills, powers, and forces at work. And thus, many things transpire in life that God does not want to happen. He has no good reason for them because He is not orchestrating them. God has entered into a covenant to respect human freedom in hopes that we will choose to use that freedom for love.

"The people of the land have practiced oppression and committed robbery, and they have wronged the poor and needy and have oppressed the sojourner without justice. I searched for a man among them who would build up the wall and stand in the gap before Me for the land, so that I would not destroy it; but I found no one" (Eze. 22:29, 30).

God longed to save the Jewish nation from the judgments that were coming upon it for its lack of humanitarian concern. His will was for them to prosper and avoid calamity. He looked for anyone who would turn the tide, but He could find no one. The same idea is found in Jeremiah's lamentations over the judgment of his people. Notice what Jeremiah said:

"For He does not afflict willingly or grieve the sons of men" (Lam. 3:33).

Have you ever gotten someone to do something that that person was unwilling to do? What is it that one individual has to exert against another in order for this to happen? A certain amount of force or pressure must be exerted. And so we find Jeremiah stating that there are some things that God does against His will because He is forced to.

Could it be that God is not choosing what to allow and what not to allow, but has instead entered into a covenant of freedom with His creation? If He is to stay true to that covenant, He is often forced against His will and placed in a position in which He doesn't want certain things to happen, desires to prevent them, and yet can't. Consider Paul's statement in the book of Romans: "For the creation was subjected to futility, not willingly" (Rom. 8:20). It wasn't against creation's will, for trees and plants do not have wills of their own, but God was forced against His will to go along with the decision that Adam had made to subject this creation to futility. All of the pain and suffering of Planet Earth has been against the will of God. It is not God's fault, but humanity's, not as individuals but as a collective whole. We will explain this next.

---

[1] "And this woman, a daughter of Abraham as she is, whom Satan has bound for eighteen long years, should she not have been released from this bond on the Sabbath day? (Luke 13:16).

[2] "And He is the radiance of His glory and the exact representation of His nature, and upholds all things by the word of His power. When He had made purification of sins, He sat down at the right hand of the Majesty on high" (Heb. 1:3).

[3] "The heavens are the heavens of the Lord, but the earth He has given to the sons of men" (Ps. 115:16).

[4] "Every good thing given and every perfect gift is from above, coming down from the Father of lights, with whom there is no variation or shifting shadow" (James 1:17).

[5] "Beloved, I pray that in all respects you may prosper and be in good health, just as your soul prospers" (3 John 1:2).

[6] "'For I know the plans that I have for you,' declares the Lord, 'plans for welfare and not for calamity, to give you a future and a hope'" (Jer 29:11).

[7] "The thief comes only to steal and kill and destroy; I came that they may have life, and have it abundantly" (John 10:10).

Chapter Nine

The Earth Belongs to the Children of Men

"Thus we see the fate of millions unborn hanging on the tongue of one man, and Heaven was silent in that awful moment!"—THOMAS JEFFERSON.

"Evil prevails when good men fail to act."—UNKNOWN.

Some have taught that before anything can happen on this planet, it must pass before the "throne of the Almighty" to receive His approval. Therefore, they deduce that nothing happens on this planet that is not allowed by God for some specific, good purpose. As I've stated previously, if this is the type of world that exists when God is in control, then heaven is going to be a pretty scary place.

But this is not at all how it works. The chaos in this world is proof positive that it is under not God's complete control but someone else's. Notice how an Old Testament poet put it: "The heaven, even the heavens, are the Lord's; but the earth He has given to the children of men" (Ps. 115:16, NKJV). The heavens belong to God, but the earth has been given to us. Remember how Jesus taught us to pray? He taught us to ask that God's will be done down here on earth as it is done up in heaven. The heavens are God's, in which His perfect will is right now being done, but here on earth, it is a different story. He gave the earth to us and to our children. He is not determining what does or doesn't transpire here on earth—we are. After all, whose will is ultimately being done down here? Don't say Satan's, because no one can truly say, "The devil *made* me do it!"[1] There is a throne in front of which everything must pass before it can happen on Planet Earth, but it's not God's throne—it's *ours*.[2] This world is our home, yet it is a home owned by a community, and many peoples' wills are determining what is done down here.

But you say, "What about the rape victim? The will of the rape victim is not done, but the will of the rapist." No, it's not fair that a free moral agent would use his freedom to hurt and take away other free moral agents' freedoms, but the Bible never teaches that what one free moral agent does to another free moral agent is always fair. The Bible does teach that what God does is always fair. If something seems "unfair," that is proof that God is not behind it.

But what about Satan; isn't he involved? Absolutely. Yet the real question we have to consider is Would Satan have the authority to afflict humanity if the first human being would not have *chosen* to give him that access? Adam gave Satan free access when he rebelled against God and aligned himself with the principles of the universe Satan was proposing. Yes, Eve was deceived, but Adam made a conscious choice. Selfishness took the place of love.[3] And the dominion that was given to Adam was surrendered to Satan. And so all that Satan has the ability and freedom to do was given to him not by God, but rather by us. You can trace all that Satan does back to a single decision made by a free moral human being.

But what role does God have in this? God will play as big a role as we allow. When Adam sinned, God did not want Satan to have access to Planet Earth. Yet God made us for love. Love requires freedom, and as we have previously learned, in order for freedom to be genuine, it must be irrevocable, even if things tend toward a way that one does not desire. So God was forced, in a way, to go along with Adam's decision. Notice how Paul put it in his letter to the Roman believers.

"For the creation was subjected to futility."

In other words, when Adam subjugated his dominion to Satan, God respected Adam's free choice and allowed the dominion to be passed on. But notice the next two words.

" . . . not willingly, but because of Him who subjected it . . ."

God allowed Adam's dominion to pass to Satan, but God did so unwillingly! God went along with the subjecting of this creation to futility only because it was Adam who truly subjected it. Yet God had foreseen this possibility and had prepared for it, as we see in the rest of the passage.

" . . . in hope that the creation itself also will be set free from its slavery to corruption into the freedom of the glory of the children of God. For we know that the whole creation groans and suffers the pains of childbirth together until now" (Rom. 8:20-22).

God had the hope that in preserving freedom rather than revoking it,

His ultimate goal could still be reached. It would be a long road, but God, through wisdom and skill, could still bring us around again to an Eden restored, the original goal experienced. Why would God grant humanity this much freedom? God made us for love, and love requires irrevocable freedom.

Yes, but once again, what about the rape victim's will? First, it would be well to remember that God made us to experience not only love with Him, but the ebb and flow of love between each other as well. God intended that Adam and Eve would love Him, and also each other. Human beings were to be bound up in the web of other-centered love, continuously and spontaneously helping and blessing each other. Yet in order for us to be enabled to experience the pleasure of freely loving each other, we must also be free to genuinely not love each other. We must be free to bestow love on our fellow members of the human race or withhold it. There is no middle ground here. We either live for others or live for ourselves. A life centered on living for oneself produces suffering for those left in the wake of the selfish individual. Even with rape you can trace that action back to the free moral decision of a human being somewhere that chose for that rape to exist in humanity's history, knowingly or unknowingly. What if the rapist was abused and therefore a victim without the power of self-mastery over their own decisions? You can trace that abuse back to a beginning somewhere, where a morally free individual could have chosen to abuse or not to abuse, either to start a trail of abuses and victims or not to.

You may still say, "What about the rape victim's will?" Any time a person chooses to violate God or others, someone's will is being violated by the free moral decision of another. I will freely admit that this is truly unfair. The Bible never states that what we do to each other is always fair; it does state that what God does is always fair. Many times what we choose to do to each other is not fair at all, but sick and evil.

God made us for the *pleasure* of love. Although love can be awakened, it cannot be coerced. The possibility of love requires that an individual be irrevocably free to love or not to love. This irrevocable freedom inadvertently and naturally creates a reality for God called risk. Notice what the author of Ecclesiastes wrote:

"I again saw under the sun that the race is not to the swift and the battle is not to the warriors, and neither is bread to the wise nor wealth to the discerning nor favor to men of ability; for time and chance overtake them all" (Eccl. 9:11).

This verse contradicts the worldview of God's being in total control. If He were, how could chance ever happen to anybody? But here it states unequivocally that chance happens to us *all*. Also, we would assume that the race is always won by the fastest, the battle always won by the strongest, sustenance is available to those who have the greatest wisdom, riches accumulate for the really smart, and favor increases for those who are gifted with amazing abilities. But the author of this verse adds a new element to the equation—chance. We exist in a world in which the outcome of events is created not only by our own choices, but also by an infinite number of other intersecting free moral decisions. This produces a chance that things won't always go the way we want, nor will they always go the way God wants.

Is there an advantage in being the fastest in a race? Absolutely, but does being the fastest guarantee victory? The Bible implies no, simply because we are not the only ones determining how things turn out. It's not that God's will is so infinitely complex that we cannot understand the good reason this evil has invaded our lives. Rather, it's because the nature of a free world, with all the millions of free decisions springing out of our God-given irrevocable freedom, is so infinitely complex that we can't possibly trace the path to the answer.

Again, God's will for us is quite simple. He never desires any of His created and infinitely loved beings to suffer, but we keep thwarting His desire with what we choose to bring into our lives and the lives of those around us.

The pleasure of love is impossible to experience without irrevocable freedom, but freedom has produced a great risk for God. Things could go the way He wants, or they could go the way He doesn't want. If they should go the way He doesn't want, a formidable struggle is created in which God must strive, labor, and earnestly endeavor to work in order for His will to be accomplished. This is where we see ourselves today. We find ourselves in a world gone wrong, a world in which God's will is often not done, a world in which a *great controversy* rages during which God must continually fight for His will to be done. Sometimes He is able to intervene and prevent tragedy; other times He is not. What determines the difference? He will show us the complete, satisfying answer one day.

I would like to close this section with a question. What assurance can we have that God will ultimately win? God is going to win, not because He's in control, but because He has an incredible amount of ability, skill, and love. Although it may be a formidable struggle, He will win because He is capable of winning—even with these odds. God will not win because He's God. God is God because He will win. What He wants will ultimately triumph.

There are four assurances God can give us in this free world. Considering the fact that there are other free moral agents in the universe besides Himself and us, He cannot guarantee that nothing bad will ever happen to us, but He can promise us that, first, He has triumphed over Satan, both at creation and at Calvary, and we can be assured that He will triumph in the end.[4] This final victory will happen not because He is controlling the outcome, but rather because He is genuinely greater in wisdom, skill, and love than His opponent. One day He will be able to bring it all to a final and complete end, and then He will wipe away every tear from our eyes.[5] And so the promise stands that this suffering will end and that God will be able to comfort and heal our hearts from our tragic history.

Second, God promises that He is going to bring evil to an end in such a way that our history of rebellion will never be repeated. This will never happen again. "Affliction will not rise up a second time" (Nahum 1:9, NKJV). This will be not because God will take away our freedom, or take away our capacity to rebel, but rather, because God will have a people who finally understand. They will realize the connection between cause and effect, as well as the fact that they have been won to a life based on the principles of love and would never choose to live any other way. This history will not be repeated, not because those who live throughout eternity *can't* rebel, but simply because they *won't*. They will realize that God did not sit down one day and arbitrarily make up some rules and say, "If you don't live by My rules, I'll pounce!" Rather, they will realize that something is wrong, not because God says so. God says something is wrong because it is. They will understand that there are certain things in the universe that naturally lead to pain, suffering, and hurt and that there are things that naturally lead to joy, peace, and happiness. Those who are living throughout eternity will also fully understand the things that bring peace and happiness, and therefore they will voluntarily and willingly choose throughout eternity to live in harmony with these principles. That is the type of universe that sounds appealing. That is the place I would like to spend the ceaseless ages of eternity.

The third assurance that God gives us is that He loves us, and therefore never does a soul hurt when He Himself does not feel our every pain. Notice the words of Jesus when He explained what God will say one day to the human race as a collective whole.

"The King will answer and say to them, 'Truly I say to you, to the extent that you did it to one of these brothers of Mine, even the least of them, you did it to Me.'. . . Then He will answer them, 'Truly I say to you, to the extent that you did not do it to one of the least of these, you did not do it to Me'" (Matt. 25:40-45).

Never has a child been molested, never a woman raped, never a person murdered, that God Himself was not molested, raped, or murdered. God is not absent in our suffering. Because of His infinite love for each of us, He feels the pain that afflicts us, much like the suffering we experience when people we care for are suffering. God loves us infinitely more than we can imagine. When we choose to abuse our freedom and hurt each other, God suffers too, as if the atrocities we do to each other were done to Him directly. With this in mind, read the above passage again. When we hurt each other, we are also hurting Him, for the greater our capacity to love others, the equally greater our capacity to hurt when they hurt. God is not behind our suffering, orchestrating evil events such as rape or child molestation for our character growth. God desires for us to experience joy, not suffering. With sensitivity God is connected to each individual, and His place is beside the victim. He also is suffering at the hands of those who are choosing to set in motion events that are contrary to what He wants. When our will is violated, His will is being violated too! So our third assurance is that we are not alone. He is *with us* in all we suffer.

Fourth and finally, God has promised that, if we will let Him, whatever others have meant for our pain, God can bring good out of it that would not have taken place otherwise.[6] Once again, a word of caution here is needed. Many times we see the good that God miraculously brings out of our suffering, and we go one step too far. At the fear of being repetitious, this must be clearly understood. We too often reason that God was somehow either orchestrating our pain or "allowing" it in order to bring about this good result. I believe that this is the most subtle and yet damaging assumption one can accept concerning the character of the One the Bible calls "love." Just because God can bring good out of evil does not mean that He ordains evil for good. This would mean that the all-good God of the universe endorses the principle of "the end justifies the means."

My wife and I were visiting a church shortly before the birth of our fourth child. We had buried our middle two as full-term stillbirths, and my wife was not looking forward to being classified as having a high-risk pregnancy, or to having our little one in the hospital. We had the privilege of having our first child at home with no complications. At the lunch following the service, she was sharing with some members how she wished she could go back to that experience. Then a well-meaning saint interjected with a pious smile, "Maybe there's someone in the hospital God wants you to meet."

I was about to let loose with a hasty response, but my wife did the wiser thing. She simply got up and walked outside into the parking lot. I quickly followed. My wife spurted out, "What did she mean by that? Does she really believe that I lost two children because God has someone in the hospital He wants me to meet? Has God really orchestrated all this loss in order for me to bump into someone in a hospital room who needs to be reached?" Whether or not that dear lady had really thought through the meaning of her reply, the implication was dastardly.

Does God really orchestrate human suffering to bring about good from the hurt? Or do bad things simply happen, and God, for those who will let Him, somehow miraculously turns it around for good? The difference is subtle but vital. Once again, when good comes out of evil we need to praise God for His ability to undo bad situations. We don't need to slander His character by saying that the "reason" for the evil event was that God was behind it, either causing or allowing it in order to bring good out of the evil.

Years after being sold into slavery by his own brothers, the Old Testament character Joseph found them kneeling at his feet in fear and repentance for their treachery. With skillful balance Joseph replied, "The evil you planned to do me has by God's design been turned to good, to bring about the present result: the survival of a numerous people" (Gen. 50:20, New Jerusalem).

Joseph did not blame God for the evil event by saying that God was working for the survival of numerous people. This would imply that God had inspired Joseph's brothers or had somehow allowed Joseph's brothers to sell Joseph for a higher reason.

Joseph glorified God for taking the evil that a group of free moral agents chose to set in motion and for bringing out of it an alternate chain of events resulting in the saving of an entire nation, and possibly, the world. Joseph was privileged to be recorded in sacred Scripture as a symbol of Christ, from whose pain the world would be saved. Yes, the evil in his life was unfortunate, but God in His mercy turned it around for good.

We may experience evil at the hands of other free moral agents, but God has promised that He will turn around all our pain and set in motion an alternate chain of events that will result in great good. This is quite a promise!

---

[1] Have you ever noticed that when tragedy strikes, God gets blamed for things He didn't do, Satan gets blamed for things he did do, and men and women eventually take the credit for things they don't even have the ability to pull off?

[2] "And God said, 'Let us make man in our image, after our likeness: and let them have dominion over the fish of the sea, and over the birds of the heavens, and over the cattle, and over all the earth, and over every creeping thing that creepeth upon the earth'" (Gen. 1:26, ASV). "Thou makest him to have dominion over the works of thy hands; thou hast put all things under his feet" (Ps. 8:6, ASV).

[3] "But I am afraid that, as the serpent deceived Eve by his craftiness, your minds should be led astray from the simplicity and purity of devotion to Christ" (2 Cor. 11:3). "And it was not Adam who was deceived, but the woman being deceived, fell into transgression" (1 Tim. 2:14).

[4] "Now judgment is upon this world; now the ruler of this world will be cast out" (John 12:31).

[5] "And He will wipe away every tear from their eyes; and . . . there will no longer be any mourning, or crying, or pain; the first things have passed away" (Rev. 21:4).

[6] "And we know that God causes all things to work together for good to those who love God, to those who are called according to His purpose" (Rom. 8:28).

Chapter Ten

The Eyes of a King

///

"I am ready to meet my Maker. Whether my Maker is prepared for the ordeal of meeting me is another matter."—WINSTON CHURCHILL.

"Oh, my soul, be prepared to meet Him who knows how to ask questions."
—T. S. ELIOT.

If you are still with me, you may have that feeling I get often. I repeatedly feel God tapping on my shoulder with a loving grin, whispering, "Maybe I'm not exactly as you have thought Me to be." Are you beginning to *see* Him a little differently, dear reader? He's not done with our hearts yet. The best is yet to unfold. Let's continue.

A long time ago, in a land far away, there lived a king like none other who had ruled before in the history of the world. This king was pure. He had no inkling toward corruption. He was kind, thoughtful, full of mercy, and yet understood the delicate balance between justice and mercy that is so vital to ruling a kingdom. This king was also wise and prudent. His intellect was broad and sharp. His heart was pure, honest, and large. His hand was firm, strong, and fair. No one had ever ruled a kingdom the way this king did. His principles showed great depth and balance of both thought and emotion. After a time it was rumored that this king was actually one of the gods who had taken human form in order to bring some type of peace to their portion of the world.

Yet no matter how just or good the king was, rebellions would break out from time to time. No one could fathom why. Was it a misunderstanding, maybe a misperception on the part of rebels concerning the goodness and superiority of their ruler? Whatever the cause, the king dealt with all rebels in the same way. He would summon them to his court and invite them into his audience chamber for one request and one request only. His desire for his rebels was simply to take into account all they had done and then look the king *in the eye*. As strange as this may sound, the king simply wanted to make eye contact with them. You see, the king had made an assumption early on. Yes, there would be uprising through jealousy and greed, but the majority of the rebellions that broke out would have to be based on misunderstandings. No one in his right mind, as long as greed was not considered, would rebel against a kingdom as balanced and purely run as this one. So the king would simply ask the rebel to look him in the eyes. He believed, as many do today, that "the eyes are a window to the soul." Looking into his eyes, rebels would see into his soul and realize that they were in the presence of a great and good ruler. They would begin to question their assumptions about the king and be won back to loyalty. The king believed that the majority of rebels could be turned, in the light of truth, back to loyal and faithful subjects once again. Many of them became advisers or top officials in the king's court and served to communicate the truth of the king to other rebels.

Yet sometimes rebellions were based not on misunderstanding but on greed and a desire for self-exaltation. The rebels knew how good the king was, and even in the light of His selfless rule, they chose to rebel out of a desire for selfish pursuits. Even so, the king's response was the same. He would invite these rebels into his presence, to stand face to face, and in the quietness of introspection to gaze into his eyes.

Legend states that one of two things would occur.

In the first outcome, the rebel would see the goodness in the soul of the king, the rebel's own character would begin to stand out in stark contrast, and his conscience would be activated. Shame for his rebellion against such a wise, selfless, and charitably pure ruler would surface, he would repent, cease his rebellion, and become a loyal subject.

In the second outcome, the rebel would not repent. The weight of his own guilt would become so intense that the psychological pressure of how out of harmony he was with the purity of the king would be more than he could bear. If left to bear the weight of his guilt alone, it would, as the legend states, crush out his life, forever ending that rebellion.

The king was renowned for not overcoming evil with evil, but with good.[1]

I believe this short story closely parallels our situation as a rebel planet living in an unfallen universe. It is hinted at, I believe, in the interchange between Moses, that great leader of God's people out of national slavery, and God on the mountain. Moses asked, "Please show me Your glory." The Lord responded by making a strange statement: "You cannot see My face; for no man shall see Me, and live" (Ex. 33:18, 20, NKJV).

Why? Is God's face such a secret—like the old spy stories where the agent would say in low tones, "I'd tell ya but I'd have to kill ya" ? Is it arbitrary, or is God simply trying to explain a natural process of cause and effect? Could it be that to look into the face of a holy God would be the same as our legendary rebel looking into the eyes of our legendary king? Could it be that to look into the eyes of God would usher us into a psychological and emotional encounter from which none of us, on our own, would survive?

Notice the experience of the ancient prophet Isaiah when he found himself in the presence of God. "Woe is me, for I am ruined! Because I am a man of unclean lips, and I live among a people of unclean lips; for my eyes have seen the King, the Lord of hosts" (Isa. 6:5). Isaiah stated that his eyes had *seen* the King, the Lord of hosts, and this *seeing* immediately made him conscious of his own uncleanness and the uncleanness of those among whom he lived. When we encounter God and are swallowed up in the vision of His holiness and purity, we immediately begin to realize how out of harmony we are with His goodness. If we, like Isaiah, were to *see* the King in his glory, we too would immediately exclaim, "Woe is me!"

Scripture records many such reactions from coming into the presence of God or into the reflection of His goodness through an angel. When Adam and Eve, Moses, Daniel, Isaiah, and even Peter in a fisherman's boat came in contact with the King of the universe, their own disharmony with the character of the King became so painfully apparent that they either cowered in fear, believing they were about to die, or immediately began to search for a way to avert their gaze and escape the presence of the One whose mere sight brought this solemn and fearful realization.

When Jesus returns to our planet, "every eye will see Him" (Rev. 1:7). The book of Revelation records the outcome: "The kings of the earth and the great men and the commanders and the rich and the strong and every slave and free man hid themselves in the caves and among the rocks of the mountains; and they said to the mountains and to the rocks, 'Fall on us and hide us from the presence of Him who sits on the throne, and from the wrath of the Lamb'" (Rev. 6:15, 16).

This verse is puzzling because of the language used. Those who are seeking to escape this encounter are asking to be hidden from God's presence and from the "wrath of the lamb," a baby sheep. When is the last time you ran from an angry *baby sheep?* It doesn't say "the wrath of the lion of Judah;" it says that they will exclaim, "Hide us . . . from the wrath of the lamb!" Strange indeed!

Adam and Eve also ran to hide from God's "presence."[2] The prophet Isaiah stated that we would "see" the King in all His beauty and, rather than joy, there would be hearts that meditate on "terror."[3]

What is this experience that seems to be so consistent in those who encounter God's purity? Scripture gives a very clear and simple explanation. The beginning of the explanation is found in the wisdom of King Solomon when he wrote, "The wicked flee when no one is pursuing" (Prov. 28:1). What is it about doing something that we know we shouldn't be doing that makes us feel as if we are being chased?

When David, ancient Israel's king-to-be, was being chased by Saul, the current and desperately wicked king, Saul entered a cave where, unbeknownst to him, David was hiding with his soldiers. In an effort to prove that his intentions were not to dethrone the king, David snuck up behind Saul and cut off a corner of the royal robe. Even though David's intentions were upright, the act of cutting the king's royal robe was unheard-of in that culture, and David's conscience began to bother him (see 1 Sam. 24:5).

At the beginning of this book we discovered that God created us to experience the pleasure of other-centered love. Yet in order for us to experience pleasure in loving others, we would have to be somehow psychologically or emotionally connected to our behavior toward others. So God created us with a conscience to connect us to our behavior toward others, making it possible to experience good feelings when we do good things for others.

This gift, however, comes with a grave risk. What if we should choose, being free moral agents, to relate with others, not positively, but negatively? In doing things we know we shouldn't, things we know are wrong, things that bring pain to others, we, being still connected psychologically to our behavior, now begin to experience pain and discomfort ourselves. This discomfort we call "a sense of guilt." When David cut off a piece of Saul's robe, his conscience smote him. Our conscience will either strike us or pat us on the back, depending on the behavior in which we choose to engage.

God did not sit back one day, decide on a bunch of rules, and say,

"You know, all these things that are fun and exciting, I think I'll make these activities wrong. And these activities that are boring, I'll make these holy, just, and good." No! Morality is not that arbitrary. I believe God looked out into the vast universe He was about to bring into existence, foresaw the possibility of things that *would cause* pain and suffering, and said, "The things that bring pain, suffering, and sadness are wrong." They are wrong, both because of what they will do to the victims of such behavior and because of the psychological results of pain and suffering they would set in motion in the transgressors themselves. Then God looked out and foresaw the possibility for things that lead to peace, joy, and happiness, and said, "These things are right and good. These things will be a blessing, and bring happiness not only to those for whom these activities are done but also for those who do them."

In a person with a healthy conscience, sin hurts not only those against whom the sin is committed but also the sinner. This is why sin is so hateful to a holy and loving God. Yes, sin is wrong, but it is wrong not because God says so. God says so because it's wrong. Sin is wrong because it hurts.

Consider what will take place in the conscience of the lost when Jesus returns. According to John, they will run to escape it. According to Solomon, they will be running when no one is chasing after them. Now let's turn our attention to Paul's explanation in the first part of his letter to the Roman believers.

"But because of your stubbornness and unrepentant heart you are *storing up wrath* for yourself in the day of wrath and *revelation* of the righteous judgment of God, who will *render* to each person *according to their deeds*. . . . There will *be tribulation and distress* for every *soul* of man who does evil. . . . All who have sinned without the Law will also *perish* without the Law. . . . For when [these] who do not have the Law do instinctively the things of the Law, these, not having the Law, are a law to themselves, in that they show the work of the Law written in their hearts, their *conscience* bearing witness and *their* thoughts alternately *accusing* or else defending them" (Rom. 2:5-15).

Notice the progression: (1) storage of wrath (2) for a day of revelation (3) when there will be a rendering (4) according to deeds, (5) the rendering being tribulation of and distress of soul, (6) which ends in perishing, (7) and all this taking place in their conscience, their own thoughts accusing them.

First, there is a storing up of wrath by a lack of repentance that will ignite through a process Paul calls "revelation." The psychological experience of intensified guilt and shame in the previous examples covered in this chapter also came as a result of "revelation," specifically the revelation of God and His purity in contrast to our disharmony with all that is altruistic and good.

Second, this revelation will render to each person a psychological experience that is in accordance with his or her deeds. Among the many definitions of "render," there are three that are worthy of mention here: (1) to portray something or somebody in art, literature, music, or acting; (2) to deliver a verdict or decision officially; (3) to purify or extract something by melting, especially to heat solid fat slowly until as much liquid fat as possible has been extracted from it, leaving small, crisp remains.

This revelation of God will also portray an accurate understanding of ourselves, as well. It will deliver, therefore, an accurate verdict. And up until this day of full disclosure and revelation, small doses of this revelatory process throughout the history of sin and sinners has had a purifying effect on many. Let me explain.

When we see God, we also see a little of ourselves. At that point we have a decision. We either hold on to what we see, which prevents God from advancing our knowledge of Himself safely, or we say, "I'd rather have restoration than this," and let the whole thing go. When we choose this option, we are ready to see more. And this process continues until restoration to love and loyalty to God and the principles upon which the universe harmoniously operates is accomplished. And so this revelation also "purifies." Thus, "render" is an extremely fitting word.

This revelation on the day of wrath will cause the lost, according to their deeds, to experience tribulation and distress of soul. Paul did not say *body*, but *soul*. This is crucial. Yes, at the end of this age,[4] there will be a physical fire in which even our earthly "elements" will melt away.[5] But I would like you to consider the cross of Jesus. Surely at Calvary we encounter an enormous amount of "physical" suffering on the part of Jesus. But if all we see is what Jesus suffered physically, we really don't have a clue what His sacrifice entailed. Jesus suffered, not only on a physical level, but on a very real and literal psychological and emotional level as well.[6]

And so it is with the final fate of the wicked. If all we understand is what they will endure on a physical level, we really have no clue what they will actually experience. Paul states that they will experience tribulation and distress on a soul level. The meaning of the original Greek words from which the English words "tribulation" and "distress" come are illustrated in the way the British penal system previously executed its criminals. They were tied to the ground facing the sky with heavy weights placed upon them until the weight crushed out their life.

Paul is telling us that the wicked will experience something so heavy that it will crush out their life. But this "tribulation and distress of soul" is not the tribulation they suffer physically. "Soul" is translated from the Greek word *psuche*. It is this Greek word from which we also get our English words "psyche," "psychology," and "psychiatry." This is talking not about the physical component of human beings, but about their mental and emotional makeup. Paul is telling us in very clear words that the wicked will suffer life-crushing distress on a very real and literal psychological and emotional level. The end result of this soul distress is that they will *perish*. The psychological distress will crush out their life. Have you ever met someone who was suffering physically because of guilt?

Next, Paul shares exactly what will be transpiring in the psyche of the lost that will end their life. They will experience the "accusation" of "their own thoughts" within their own "conscience." When we engage in negative acts, these acts set guilt and shame in motion that, according to Paul, is intensified in the presence or sight of God to the point of being life threatening. This is why no one can see the face of God and live.

I had a friend in high school who in exasperation blurted out, "Why do you love the Bible? All I get when I read that book is confused and mixed up. If I were God, I would have written it a lot simpler. If I were a God who was good and wanted to clear up the misunderstanding concerning Himself, I would have put it as clear as day—simply—so that a person could get it at first glance." I pondered my friend's statement for years, and one day God's dilemma dawned on me. We need to encounter the truth concerning God's character in order to be restored. We need to see God! But because we have sinned and are now exposed to guilt and shame, the revelation of God's character will not save us, but will ignite a psychological process of cause and effect that will end in our death. If God is not careful, the very thing that will save us will destroy us instead. So God has to reveal Himself to us in slow, safe doses, while enabling us to encounter a little bit of Himself and ourselves at a time. Then He provides the options of confession, repentance, and faith in God's forgiveness to remove the guilt, allowing us to go further in our understanding of God's goodness. If God were to give us the full revelation of His pure goodness in such a way that we would encounter it fully upon first glance in Scripture, would we be able to handle it? No, we would perish in the encounter because of the obvious disharmony between our self-centeredness and the complete other-centeredness of God. This is why God had to distance Himself physically from the beginning. Notice how it worked for Adam and Eve. Just the mere sensing of God's presence caused them to run and hide under feelings of fear and nakedness—running away while no one was chasing them.

In the last book of the Bible John explains this same phenomenon in his vision concerning the white throne judgment.

"Then I saw a great white throne and Him who sat upon it, from whose presence earth and heaven fled away, and no place was found for them" (Rev. 20:11).

Notice that the presence of God is once again the catalyst. Either there is no place in heaven or earth for those who have rebelled to hide so that they can escape, or they are so out of harmony with God's goodness that, as they look around, there is no place in the universe where they fit in or belong. Their own disharmony with the principles of other-centeredness has unfitted them for habitation in a future brought back into balance with these principles. Could it be that these rebels are not allowed into the happy home of the restored, where all is unselfish and pure, because their conscience would so continuously torture them for their disharmonious self-centeredness that the new heavens and new earth would actually be a place of *eternal torment* for them?

John continues. "And I saw the dead, the great and the small, standing before the throne, and books were opened; and another book was opened, which is the book of life; and the dead were judged from the things which were written in the books, according to their deeds" (verse 12).

In the presence of God the lost will experience an awakening of full consciousness to the disclosure of each event of their lives and whether they lived in harmony with what is other-centered and loving or aligned with all that is self-centered and harmful. They will begin to perceive judgment according to how they've lived their lives. God is not arbitrarily pronouncing judgment on individuals who simply have not played by His rules. The lost will experience the natural, internal effect of how they have lived. Consider how Paul describes the judgment that sin brings.

"All who have sinned without the Law will also perish without the

Law, and all who have sinned under the Law will be judged . . . [according to what's written in] the Law; for it is not the hearers of the Law who are just before God, but the doers of the Law will be justified. [The opposite of being justified is being condemned. Now, notice what will condemn the lost, who have not had the law.] For when Gentiles who do not have the Law do instinctively the things of the Law, these, not having the Law, are a law to themselves, in that they show the work [or workings of, or what the law produces] of the Law written in *their hearts*, their *conscience* bearing witness and *their thoughts alternately accusing or else defending them*" (Rom. 2:12-15).

Paul is saying that on the day described by John, we will be judged, either condemned or justified, according to our deeds, and the agent through which we experience condemnation or justification is *our conscience*. Whether or not an individual has an overactive conscience or a deadened conscience, on that day, in the presence of God, our consciences will be quickened, or made alive. If we are out of harmony with what we know to be good, the only experience awaiting us is psychological and emotional condemnation.

Yet the careful thinker will realize that every single one of us is a rebel. On our own we are all destined for this life-crushing experience "in the sight of " or "when we see" God, for "no one can see His face and live." Yet God offers us a solution—the only solution. We can experience justification, even though we are sinners destined for condemnation. Regardless of our past lives, there is a way in which we can experience psychological and emotional peace in God's presence, even though we are sinners and rebel. This peace, this psychological justification rather then condemnation, God shares with us through the miracle of *faith*. We will discuss faith in more detail in the next few chapters as we take a practical look at the gospel of Jesus.

John discusses the fate of the lost in another passage. Since Revelation is a symbolic book, this description is also highly symbolic— wine, a cup, fire and brimstone, a lamb, a beast, an image, a mark, and an eternally rising smoke. Amid all of these symbols, one thing is clear—the catalyst of the torment is once again the presence of God.

"He also will drink of the wine of the wrath of God, which is mixed in full strength in the cup of His anger; and he will be tormented with fire and brimstone in the *presence* of the holy angels and in the *presence* of the Lamb. And the smoke of their torment goes up forever and ever; they have no rest day and night, those who worship the beast and his image, and whoever receives the mark of his name" (Rev. 14:10, 11).

When John states that the lost will experience an inability to experience rest, he is actually quoting from the famous words of Moses known to many as "the blessings and the cursings."

"Among those nations you shall find no rest, and there will be no resting place for the sole of your foot; but there the Lord will give you a trembling heart, failing of eyes, and despair of soul. So your life shall hang in doubt before you; and you will be in dread night and day, and shall have no assurance of your life. In the morning you shall say, 'Would that it were evening!' And at evening you shall say, 'Would that it were morning!' because of the dread of your heart which you dread, and for the sight of your eyes which you will see" (Deut. 28:65-67).

This psychological and emotional dread and torment is the result of the "sight" of their "eyes." As they encounter God, they also begin to encounter themselves. The awakening of their own understanding of the goodness and other-centeredness of God's character and how out of harmony their own characters are awakens an equally proportionate amount of guilt and shame. Regardless of whether a person's disharmony with holiness is little or great, the slightest bit of disharmony with His goodness fills the heart with such a great mental weight of guilt, shame, and condemnation that his life is crushed out. Look closely at the following illustration.

Glory ⟶ **Sin** ⟶ **Torment/Wrath** ⟶ **Death**

This chain reaction is set in motion by the full disclosure of the light of God's other-centered love, for "everything exposed by the light becomes visible, for it is light that makes everything visible" (Eph. 5:13, 14, NIV). This light is the radiance of the true revelation of the character of God, whether reflected in the lives of God's people or by angels, Jesus, or the Father Himself. Therefore it was to reveal God, in such a way as to save us from sin and guilt, that Jesus came to live among humanity. Just as humanity's fall came as a result of deception concerning the character of God, so humanity's restoration would come as a result of having a true understanding of God's character. Yet Jesus had to reveal the Father in such a way as to save us, not destroy us. This is where we turn our attention in the next few chapters—the coming of a Savior.

[1] "Do not be overcome by evil, but overcome evil with good" (Rom. 12:21).

[2] "They heard the sound of the Lord God walking in the garden in the cool of the day, and the man and his wife hid themselves from the presence of the Lord God among the trees of the garden" (Gen. 3:8).

[3] "Your eyes will see the King in His beauty; they will behold a far-distant land. Your heart will meditate on terror" (Isa. 33:17, 18).

[4] "So just as the tares are gathered up and burned with fire, so shall it be at the end of the age" (Matt. 13:40).

[5] "But the day of the Lord will come like a thief, in which the heavens will pass away with a roar and the elements will be destroyed with intense heat, and the earth and its works will be burned up" (2 Peter 3:10).

[6] "About the ninth hour Jesus cried out with a loud voice, saying, 'Eli, Eli, lama sabachthani?' that is, 'My God, My God, why have You forsaken Me?'" (Matt. 27:46).

Chapter Eleven

. . . From Their Sins

"We are punished by our sins, not for them."—ELBERT HUBBARD.

Way back in the beginning of this race's history God lovingly warned Adam and Eve of the danger of sin and the chain of events that sin would set in motion. We pick up this dialogue through the writings of Moses: "The Lord God commanded the man, saying, 'From any tree of the garden you may eat freely; but from the tree of the knowledge of good and evil you shall not eat, for in the day that you eat from it you will surely die'" (Gen. 2:16, 17).

It is interesting to note that God did not threaten them: "If you eat the fruit, I'll kill you." He wanted them to understand that by eating the fruit, they would be setting in motion a chain of events that would ultimately end in death.

I have a friend who said, "I can't serve a God who says, 'Serve me or I'll kill you.'" I responded, "My dear friend, God isn't saying, 'Serve me or I'll kill you.' He's saying, 'You're dying: let Me make you live!'"

James put it this way: "But each one is tempted when he is drawn away by his own desires and enticed. Then, when desire has conceived, it gives birth to sin; and sin, when it is full-grown, brings forth death" (James 1:14, 15, NKJV). There is a progression of events here that ends in death.

Paul describes this progression in his letter to the believers in Rome (Rom. 7). Let's look at it one section at a time.

"While we were living in the flesh, our sinful passions, aroused by the law, were at work in our members to bear fruit for death" (Rom. 7:5, RSV).

When we see God's glory, we also see our own sin. Seeing these two simultaneously produces a psychological and emotional torment the Bible calls wrath, which, if we were left to bear it in full, would end in our death.

Glory ⟶ **Sin** ⟶ **Torment/Wrath** ⟶ **Death**

Paul is pointing out this same progression. When we were "in the flesh," our sinful passions (sin) were aroused by the law (awakened by the revelation of that which is good and holy, the law simply being a transcript of God's other-centered character, or *glory*). Being aroused by an encounter with holiness, our sinful passions began bearing a fruit that produces death. This fruit is guilt, shame, and a sense of condemnation, which, if we were left to bear it alone, would produce death in us. Let's continue with Paul's logic.

"What then should we say? That the law is sin? By no means!" (verse 7, NRSV).

Is the holy other-centeredness of God the problem? Is God and His law the problem? Paul responds with a strong no! For angels and other unfallen beings dwell continually in God's holy presence, ever surrounded by His other-centered love, and for them the presence is life–giving. Why is it so different for us? The answer is obvious—we have sinned and thus have guilt.

"Yet, if it had not been for the law, I would not have known sin" (verse 7, NRSV).

The realization of the other-centered love of God creates in us a keen self-awareness of our self-centered sinfulness by contrast.

"I was once alive apart from the law, but when the commandment came, sin revived and I died" (verses 9, 10, NRSV).

Once again, when we see God, there comes home to the conscience an awareness of our own sin, and guilt and shame become all-consuming. The end result is that we die.

"And the very commandment that promised life proved to be death to me" (verse 10, NRSV).

God's other-centered love was intended only to be the source of life for the universe, yet the mystery of sin causes contact with God's other-centeredness to have contrary results. This is why sin is so hateful to a holy God. It hurts and ultimately kills the objects of His affection whom He lovingly created for love, joy, happiness, and peace. Sin makes it impossible for them, on their own, to live in His presence ever again.

"For sin, seizing an opportunity in the commandment, deceived me and through it killed me. So the law is holy, and the commandment is holy and just and good. Did what is good, then, bring death to me? By no means! It was sin, working ["producing" (New King James Version)] death in me through what is good" (verses 11-13, NRSV).

Sin seizes the opportunity through the commandment's relation to the conscience and produces the fruit of guilt, which, if we were left to bear it alone, would crush out our life. Thus, sin produces death in us, "through what is good." Notice how Paul phrased this process in his letter to the believers in Galatia.

"Do not be deceived: God cannot be mocked. A man reaps what he sows. The one who sows to please his sinful nature, from that nature will reap destruction; the one who sows to please the Spirit, from the Spirit will reap eternal life" (Gal. 6:7, 8, NIV).

Did you catch the sources for both destruction and eternal life? According to Paul they are not the same. We reap what we sow. In agriculture, if you plant perennials, you will *from that seed* have flowers that will return each year. If you plant annuals, you will *from that seed* have flowers that will last only one season. What you sow determines what is produced. It's the seed from which the flower grows, and it is the seed that makes the difference.

Here's another example. If I plant an apple seed, it is perfectly accurate to say that the great tree that grows as a result came from the very seed that I planted. The only reason I did not end up with an orange tree is because I planted an apple seed and not an orange seed. Paul taps into this agricultural example by stating that if we sow to please our self-centered natures, we will, *from that self-centered nature,* reap destruction. But if we sow to please the other-centered Spirit of God, we will, *from that Spirit,* reap eternal life. Death comes *from* our self-centered natures, while eternal life comes *from* the Spirit.

Solomon agreed: "But he who sins against me injures himself" (Prov. 8:36).

We do not obey God's laws in order to be good people who earn eternal life by our behavior. God in His wisdom and mercy has simply shared insight into the way things work. The great system of cause and effect has been opened before us, and God is simply sharing with us the secrets of happiness and life. When we make choices contrary to what God has asked, we are working against not only God but also ourselves.[1]

When God warned Adam and Eve not to eat of one particular tree in their garden home, He was not stating that death would be what Adam and Eve would do to someone else or what someone else would inflict on them. He was simply stating that when they ate of the tree they would be bringing death upon themselves. All of what we have discussed in this and the previous chapter can readily be seen in the remainder of the story, found in the third chapter of Genesis.

"Then the eyes of both of them were opened, and they knew that they were naked" (Gen. 3:7).

Adam and Eve immediately began to feel the guilt, shame, and sense of condemnation that sin produces. Feelings of internal exposure and nakedness began to exhibit their effect. As a result, "they sewed fig leaves together and made themselves loin coverings" (verse 7). Thinking they could fix their psychological and emotional dilemma through covering their physical nakedness, they immediately began to negotiate with their conscience through externals.

How many times do we try to cleanse the guilt from our conscience through an endless round of duties related to our crime? We try to undo the past through present endeavors. Yet for Adam and Eve, as well as for us, the guilt and shame would only intensify.

"They heard the sound of the Lord God walking in the garden in the cool of the day, and the man and his wife hid themselves from the presence of the Lord God among the trees of the garden" (verse 8).

God had said they would die. And now, built upon a foundation of wrongly perceiving God's character, they thought God was coming to kill them. As we have already seen: "The wicked flee when no one is pursuing" (Prov. 28:11). From the Garden of Eden all the way to Jesus' second coming,[2] humanity has been running from God when there is "no one chasing after them." Notice that it is God's *presence* from which the man and his wife were hiding. We as humans are plagued by the guilt and condemnation that our sins produce in our psyche. Ever since Adam and Eve, we've been running from God every time He shows up. Our feelings of guilt have made us think He's against us when really He's not. All along, we've been running when there is no one "pursuing." God is not against us; God loves us. He has never harbored any ill feelings toward us. Calvary proves it. Rather than being angry with us for how we have related to Him (and He has every right to be), God has forgiven us.[3]

I remember an old man named Mr. Wadsworth. When I was growing up, everyone in the neighborhood was afraid of him. We use to sneak past his scary-looking house into his backyard and help ourselves to the apples on his apple tree. One day I was there alone grabbing an apple when I felt a heavy hand on my shoulder. I turned around, and there was Mr. Wadsworth! I let out a scream and took off running.

Later that evening Mr. Wadsworth showed up at my house with a bag of apples. I was so embarrassed. My parents invited him to stay for dinner, and we were best friends from that day forward. I was totally wrong about Mr. Wadsworth. He was actually very cool.

Looking back on this incident makes me wonder: "Could we be wrong about God, as well?" Maybe God isn't what we think He is. God says, "You thought that I was altogether like you."[4] But He isn't! To our surprise, "God is love" (1 John 4:8). God is not the enemy; sin is! We do not need be afraid of God; we need to be afraid of sin! Nonetheless, many today will continue to react to God's pursuing love the same way that Adam and Eve did, with fear, shame, and running in an attempt to hide. How did God respond to the first couple's hiding? The all-knowing God began with a question.

"Then the Lord God called to the man, and said to him, 'Where are you?'" (Gen. 3:9).

Now, wait a minute! Did God really not know where they were hiding? Of course He knew! God knew the exact address of the bush behind which Adam and Eve were crouched. Then why did He ask? I believe that God asked this question not in an effort to obtain information but rather for the purpose of communicating and imparting information vital to Adam and Eve at that crucial moment. Before they had actually eaten the fruit, Adam and Eve believed and embraced a wrong picture of what God was like. They were both working from this picture in relating to Him. They believed the serpent's interpretation of what God was like, so their thoughts and feelings toward God were now different, causing them to relate to and experience God differently. Yet God is patient. He simply asked them where they were. And I believe that this question was asked for the purpose of letting Adam and Eve hear the tone of His voice in hopes that they would hear a contrast between what He is really like and what they perceived Him to be like. If human beings are going to be saved from sin, the act of saving must begin where sin began, with their picture of what God is like.

God began with first things first. Notice the tone of His voice. Adam and Eve were expecting a God who would show up and, like some angry parents I've witnessed, yell, "Adam! Where are you? . . . Get out here this instant! Well, if I . . . I *never* . . . You should be ashamed of yourself!" But instead of anger, they heard heartbreak. They heard pathos. They heard the heart of a God longing for them to return. They could hear the tears in His voice and imagined them running down His cheeks. They began to picture Him with outstretched arms longing to embrace them once again and gather them back into His love.

How do we know all this? Well, how did Adam and Eve respond? If God had come in anger, like an angry parent, yelling and screaming, I'm sure Adam would have found a better hiding place. Instead, Adam and Eve heard something in the tone of God's voice that made them feel that it was *safe* to come out of hiding. Adam stepped out before God. And now dialogue began.

Adam explained, "I heard the sound of You in the garden, and I was afraid because I was naked; so I hid myself" (verse 10).

And notice how God responded.

"Who told you that you were naked?" (verse 11).

Dear reader, have you ever sinned? What a silly question. Of course you have. We all have. And so we understand something of the psychological and emotional experience of Adam and Eve at this moment—feelings of shame and exposure. From whom did Adam and Eve believe these feelings were coming? Have you ever felt guilty and condemned? In the midst of condemnation, don't we all feel as if these feelings are coming from God? Have you ever been tempted to think that God actually condemned you? Remember, God condemns sin, not the sinner. God convicts the sinner, but never condemns. If God were to condemn us for one moment, we would all be dead! But we are not. God continues to cause the rain to fall on the just and the unjust. Every breath we breathe, every drop of sunshine, and every bite of food is the gracious gift of God. He continues to treat us as we don't deserve, treating each one as if we have never sinned. Matter of fact, God never has treated you like a sinner. God has treated you as if you were holy, blameless, and perfect before Him in love.

God's point in asking them who it was who told them they were naked was to show that this was not coming from Him directly but rather from their own conscience.[5] Pay attention to the next question: "Have you eaten from the tree of which I commanded you not to eat?" (verse 11). What was it that was making them feel condemned? What was it that was causing their conscience to plague them with guilt, shame, and feelings of nakedness? They had eaten of the tree. God does not kick us when we are down. Sin, or rather the disharmony with what we know or sense to be right, produces in our conscience the sensations of guilt and condemnation. If we were left to bear the full weight of the guilt and condemnation all by ourselves, the cross proves that it would crush out our lives. Remember what God told Moses as discussed in the last chapter: no one can see God and live. To see God is to become keenly aware of our own disharmony with Him, and to set in motion the chain of events of guilt, shame, and finally death. As Paul named it, to see God is to set in motion the "law of sin and of death" (Rom. 8:2).

Paul also tried to share this reality with the believers in Thessalonica regarding the outcome of God's second return. Keep in mind John's description in Revelation 6 and the story of God's appearance in Eden as you read this passage.

"These shall be punished with everlasting destruction from the presence of the Lord and from the glory of His power" (2 Thess. 1:9, NKJV).

Young's Literal Translation puts it, "Who shall suffer justice—destruction age-during—from the face of the Lord, and from the glory of his strength."

The first translation uses the word "presence," which reminds us of Adam and Eve and how sin caused them to respond to God's presence. In Eden the presence of God was tempered so as not to fully destroy, for Jesus had veiled His glory even then.[6] The second translation of this passage uses the word "face," which reminds us of God's words to Moses. To see God's glory is to come face to face with the realization of what God is and likewise what we are.

I must admit that this description of punishment, and a destruction that will never be undone, sounds quite scary, and certainly there are things we should fear regarding that day. But let me be quick to repeat that God is not the cause of our fear—*sin is!* God is not the enemy—*sin is!* God is not the one from whom we need to be saved—we need to be saved from *sin!* Over and over Scripture makes this point.

"For the wage paid by sin is death; the gift freely given by God is eternal life in Christ Jesus our Lord" (Rom. 6:23, New Jerusalem).

You readily see that three things are compared in this passage. First, Paul would like us to see the difference between the results of sin and the results of following God: "death" versus "eternal life." Next, there is the comparison of "wages" in contrast to a "gift." Finally, Paul would like us to consider the difference between God and sin. The gift of life comes from God, and the wage of death is paid out, or comes, *from* sin. Jesus came to liberate us from sin's life-crushing guilt through the revelation of the forgiveness of God. This revelation, rather than destroying us, can heal our misconceptions of His character, while simultaneously setting us free from the guilt and condemnation of our rebellion against Him. The Bible clearly states that when Christ came to this planet, His purpose was not to appease an angry God, but rather to save us from what our sins were doing to us.

"She will bear a Son; and you shall call His name Jesus, for He will save His people *from their sins*" (Matt. 1:21).

"How much more, then, will the blood of Christ, who through the eternal Spirit offered himself unblemished to God, *cleanse our consciences from acts that lead to [or produce] death,* so that we may serve the living God!" (Heb. 9:14, NIV).

"Baptism, which corresponds to this, *now saves you*, not as a removal of dirt from the body but as an appeal to God for a *clear conscience*, through the resurrection of Jesus Christ" (1 Peter 3:21, RSV).

"And baptism, of which this is an image, now gives you salvation, not by washing clean the flesh, but by *making you free from the sense of sin before God*, through the coming again of Jesus Christ from the dead" (verse 21, Basic English).

All of the above verses clearly state that we are being saved from the terrible psychological and emotional effects of our sin. The cross was not intended to win God's favor, or to appease His wrath; it was the only means through which God, in His infinite wisdom, could save us from sin.

Think back to when you have wronged someone and you could not look that person in the eye. Did reconciliation ever take place? Are you able to look him or her in the eye today? If so, what happened that enabled you to do this? If you will consider it carefully, the answer becomes obvious. That person forgave you, and you accepted his or her forgiveness. If you have ever experienced this from either side, you have a window into understanding the purpose of the cross.

Before we discuss how forgiveness leads to reconciliation, I would like you simply to consider the words of Paul to the believers in Ephesus: "In Him we have redemption through His blood, the forgiveness of our trespasses, according to the riches of His grace" (Eph. 1:7).

Notice that what we have through the cross (the shed blood of

Jesus) is redemption. Redemption is purchasing or ransoming someone from someone else who has kidnapped him. It means setting someone free at a price.

Whom does the Bible identify as the kidnapper? Yes, God paid a price in order to redeem us, but many have asked, "Whom did God pay?" Many times we get the wrong answers because we ask the wrong questions. Try asking "What did He pay?" Notice how the Bible explains this transaction. In Paul's letter to Titus we find this statement: "Who gave Himself for us to redeem us *from every lawless deed*, and to purify for Himself a people for His own possession, zealous for good deeds" (Titus 2:14).

You see, Paul's point is that God did not purchase us back from a person; rather, He purchased us from our sins. He paid what was necessary to save us psychologically and emotionally from our transgressions. When we have committed some type of violation, the cause-and-effect chain reaction of guilt and condemnation is immediately set in motion. For some violations the way we are set at liberty from that sense of guilt is to go back and undo what was done. Let me illustrate.

When I was a new driver, my parents purchased for me a white 1988 Honda CRX. I loved it because I was going to school at the time, and this car, although it was only a two-seater, got 50 miles to the gallon. As a young person who did not yet have a spouse or kids, I was meticulous about having a clean car. (My kids have almost broken me of that.) One day as I was driving down the road, I looked down at the passenger-side floorboard and noticed an empty Snickers bar wrapper. Now, before you start wondering what I was doing eating a Snickers bar, don't miss the point. I picked up the empty wrapper and began to contemplate how to get rid of it as quickly as possible. Looking at each of my rearview mirrors to make sure no one was around, I began to roll down my window when I heard a little voice inside me say, "Uh, excuse me, Herb, this is your conscience speaking. *Don't do it!*" So I rolled the window down and said to myself, "OK, I won't throw this out the window. I'll just stick it out the window and play with it!" Have you ever played games with your conscience?

I put my left hand out of the car window holding on to this empty wrapper and began to literally move it back and forth until . . . *whoosh!* The wind caught it and away it flew. I instinctively looked in my rearview mirror and said out loud, "Oh, whoops." My conscience then ceased its gentle warning, switched on the loudspeaker, and blared in my head, "Herb Montgomery, you are a litterer!"

Have you ever been there? Have you ever had your conscience smite you for something you've done that you know you shouldn't have done? This is a very powerful encounter. The weight of guilt and condemnation placed upon us by our conscience can be so powerful that it can make us do some pretty strange things. Have you experienced it? It can be an intense experience. I'll tell you how intense it can be: two miles down the road I had to turn the car around, and spent the next two hours combing the roadside for an empty Snickers bar wrapper. Once I found it I picked it up and placed it on the floorboard, exactly where it had been cluttering my car two hours previously. You may laugh at me, but this was the only way I could get my conscience to stop bothering me!

Even though this story is comical, there is a serious question that rises to the surface. "Don't you wish that everything you did in your past that plagues you with guilt were as easy to undo as simply picking up a piece of paper and throwing it in the garbage?"

Life is not that easy. There are some things that are impossible to correct. They simply cannot be undone. And so what is our result? Are we left to be plagued by guilt for the rest our lives? Are we left alone to bear the weight of guilt upon our shoulders indefinitely?

There is a solution. There is a way to be free. Follow me into the next chapter.

---

[1] "For the waywardness of the naive will kill them, and the complacency of fools will destroy them" (Prov. 1:32).

[2] "The sky was split apart like a scroll when it is rolled up, and every mountain and island were moved out of their places. Then the kings of the earth and the great men and the commanders and the rich and the strong and every slave and free man hid themselves in the caves and among the rocks of the mountains; and they said to the mountains and to the rocks, 'Fall on us and hide us from the presence of Him who sits on the throne, and from the wrath of the Lamb; for the great day of their wrath has come, and who is able to stand?'" (Rev. 6:14-17).

[3] "For if our heart condemns us, God is greater than our heart, and knows all things" (1 John 3:20, NKJV). "When you were dead in your transgressions and the uncircumcision of your flesh, He made you alive together with Him, having forgiven us all our transgressions" (Col 2:13).

[4] "These things you have done and I kept silence; you thought that I was just like you; I will reprove you and state the case in order before your eyes" (Ps. 50:21).

[5] "In that they show the work of the Law written in their hearts, their conscience bearing witness and their thoughts alternately accusing or else defending them" (Rom. 2:15).

"It came about afterward that David's conscience bothered him because he had cut off the edge of Saul's robe (1 Sam. 24:5).

[6] "Now, Father, glorify Me together with Yourself, with the glory which I had with You before the world was" (John 17:5).

Chapter Twelve

The Sufferings of a God

///

"The weak can never forgive. Forgiveness is the attribute of the strong."
—MAHATMA GANDHI.

"He who has seen me has seen the Father."—JESUS (JOHN 14:9).

My family and I used to live four miles south of the Canadian border in the northeastern region of Washington State. The nearest grocery store in the States was about an hour away, but the nearest grocery store in Canada was only 20 minutes. Suffice it to say that all of our groceries had both English and French writing on the labels. One day, as my wife and I were shopping in Canada, we met a young man who happened to be Muslim. Over time he and I became friends. One day as we were talking he asked me quite bluntly, "Herb, you're a Christian, right?"

Now, I'm not ashamed of being a Christian, but I am sometimes embarrassed at how we as Christians have represented what that means. So I very reluctantly said, "Yes, but I may not define that the way you do."

Next he asked, "Let's say that you lived in the state of Texas, and you were found guilty of first-degree murder. You were placed on death row. And then your wife appealed to the judicial system of that state and said, 'Because of my great love for Herb, why don't you let me go to the electric chair for him?' My friend then looked me straight in the eye and asked, "What answer would be given by the judicial and penal systems of Texas?" I had to admit that they would deny her request.

He then pressed me for a why, and I repeated the cliché, "He who does the crime does the time."

Shaking his head, he said, "Yet you, as a Christian, teach that Jesus, the one who was innocent, died for you, the guilty, don't you? And you also teach that one innocent man died for the sins of the entire world!" I looked at him, understanding his quandary with Christian theology. I told him that I myself had struggled with these very thoughts, and agreed that if I was *looking* at it the way he was, I would have a problem too. But that is not the way I see the cross.

I asked him to imagine that 1,000 people had stolen money from him, and upon discovery of how much had been stolen by each person, he somehow rose above the violation and frankly forgave every last one of them. Then I asked him, "In that scenario, how many people would suffer punishment for what they did?"

He said, "None."

I quickly responded, "No; there is *one* person who would suffer for what he did!" He scratched his head. Follow closely as I share with you the truths that set my friend's heart free that day. Not only was his question answered, but in the process He found His Savior.

The nature of a violation is that one party inflicts loss against an unwilling recipient. We have a violator (let's call her Nancy), and a violated (we'll call him Ted).

Ted has two options: (1) He can appeal to a higher power, such as civil government, and ask for a reasonable level of loss to be inflicted on Nancy so that fairness can be restored. This wouldn't necessarily be revenge, but restitution. Thus, Nancy (the violator) would be prosecuted. (2) Or Ted can rise above the loss inflicted upon him and willingly choose to bear whatever loss was inflicted as a result. Nancy would thus be let off the hook and be forgiven.

In both options, justice must be maintained. In option 1, it would be unjust if, when Ted calls for Nancy to be punished, someone else is punished instead. If someone other than nancy is punished the balance, equality, and fairness are not achieved. Many times Christians have given the impression that God (the violated) demands our (the violators) punishment. Yet, because He loves us so much, He sent His only Son to be punished in our place. If this were true, it would be problematic on many levels and would be unjust, to say the least, according to the principle that "he who does the crime does the time."

In the second option, it would also be unjust if someone other than Ted let Nancy go free against his will. And so we are met with a challenge. On both sides we must resist injustice. The solution must be both just and merciful. According to the Christian gospel, the end result is that the violator (us) goes free. But how do we escape the injustice of it?

In our illustration, if Nancy is going to be let off the hook it's going to come at a price to Ted. Ted will have to choose to willingly bear whatever loss was inflicted by Nancy and relinquish his right of restitution. This must be voluntarily chosen by Ted, because it will come at a price to him. There is no such thing as forgiveness that doesn't cost the forgiver something. Notice that the decision to let us (the violators) go free was not made by someone else against the will of God. God Himself embraced the loss, chose to bear our sins against Him, and chose to let us go free. In a word, this is forgiveness. Calvary is as if God, with open arms, is saying to the world, "The charges have been dropped!"

This begs the question: Was our debt to God repaid, or forgiven?

Our sin is either forgiven or repaid—but it cannot be both. And yet Scripture uses the language of both. How are we to make sense of this? We must abandon a three-party substitutionary atonement model if we are to begin to understand the nature of forgiveness. God forgave our sins against Him—someone else did not repay Him the debt. There is no such thing as forgiveness that doesn't cost the forgiver something. Did it cost God something to forgive us? Is there a cost to forgiving someone who has wronged us? Absolutely! But it must be remembered that this is not payment being *received* by the one doing the forgiving but is payment being *made* by the one doing the forgiving. This is why we see God on the cross—not us. God, the violated party, realized the injustice done, realized the personal cost to forgive, and willingly bore all out of love so that you and I, the violators, could go free.

But what about justice? you may ask. Yes, we must include justice if the picture is to be complete. In the case of my Muslim friend, if he should rise above the infliction of all those who had stolen money from him there would still be one person who would suffer: him, the violated. Yet something has changed. Instead of someone else letting them all off the hook and dropping the charges, they are being freed voluntarily and willingly by my friend himself. No third party is inno-cently stepping in and substituting themselves in the place of the guilty ones. Nor is someone else letting them off the hook unjustly. Rather, the violated party himself is choosing to bear the loss, putting himself in the place of the violators. And justice can't say a word. For it is the right of the violated to drop charges if they so choose. No one else can let the violators off the hook—only the violated, and that only voluntarily, for it will cost him everything.

This is still an act of substitution, but it is a type of substitution that is
legally acceptable and just. It is forgiveness. The violated willingly and
voluntarily putting himself in the place of all the violators, willingly bearing what was done against him, so that the violators can go free.

This is exactly how Jesus sought to explain the act of Calvary.

In one of His parables Jesus talks about a creditor and two debtors.

One debtor owed a very large sum; the other a pittance. Notice
what the creditor did:

"And when they [the two debtors] had nothing to pay, he [their credi-
tor] frankly forgave them both" (Luke 4:72, KJV).

It does not say that the creditor went out and found someone else to
pay their debt off for them. Rather, He simply forgave. Did it cost the
creditor something to forgive? Yes! But notice who paid. The creditor!
This is exactly what we see taking place at Calvary. Calvary was not the
means whereby God could forgive us if we did something first. It was the
very act of divine forgiveness itself. After all is said and done, what do we
see transpiring to the violator and the violated at the cross? We see the violator being released voluntarily by the violated, and the violated willingly
bearing the loss that should have been paid by the violator. Jesus is not
some third party, He is the violated one Himself, for Jesus is God. Notice
the following statements that Jesus made throughout His life.

"I and the Father are one" (John 10:30).

"Don't you believe that I am in the Father, and that the Father is
in me? The words I say to you are not just my own. Rather, it is
the Father, living in me, who is doing his work" (John 14:10, NIV).

Jesus said to him, "Have I been so long with you, and yet you have
not come to know Me, Philip? He who has seen Me has seen the
Father" (verse 9).

From these statements we readily see Jesus' relation to His Father.
God did not send someone else. God Himself came in the person of Jesus
Christ. This idea answers the question so often asked: "If God loves us,
why didn't He come Himself? Why send His Son?" God *did* give Himself
in the person of His Son.

This oneness also gives us more insight into what Calvary was about
and what it was not about. Some would have us believe that Calvary was
Jesus paying back the Father for our sins. Yet since Jesus and the Father
are one, this makes no sense. I remember the first birthday I spent with
my wife after we got married. Do you share a checking account with your

spouse? For various reasons we do. My wife and I are financially "one." Yet my birthday came before I really understood this aspect of marriage.

As the date was getting closer, my wife asked me what I wanted for my birthday. And being raised as an only child, I was well experienced in making a birthday list. I set about creating a categorized list of what I wanted for my first birthday as a married man.

The day came, and as we were at the party unwrapping presents, it dawned on me that I had received everything on my list. I thought, *Wow! I have married the most incredible woman in the world! She's better than Mom!*

Then it struck me. I turned to my wife and out of curiosity asked her, "By the way dear, which account did you use for all this?"

She very lovingly looked back at me and stated, "Oh, I used our joint account. That's OK, isn't it?"

It became painfully obvious to me that my wife was not the only one who had purchased these birthday presents for me. You see, since she and I are financially "one," whatever either one of us does financially, the other one does it as well. Whatever decisions we make, they implicate both of us. We are one.

Let's say you stole $1,000 from me, but my wife intervenes. With our joint checkbook in hand, she says to you, "Oh, don't worry, I'll pay Herb back for you." She then writes me a check for $1,000 from our joint checkbook, signs the check, and hands it to me. What's the problem? When the dust settles and the check clears, I'm still out $1,000. I've received nothing.

The same principle applies to God and Jesus. Jesus and the Father are one. Whatever we see Jesus doing, the Father is doing as well. Did the Father pay Himself back? If the Father, in Christ, was paying Himself back, in reality He has received nothing in repayment for our sins, for He was both paying and receiving.

If Calvary wasn't about payment but was an act of forgiveness, we use the word "payment," but in an entirely different context. Does it cost you something when you forgive? Of course! Remember, there is no such thing as forgiveness that doesn't cost the forgiver something. Your willingness to forgive is simply a statement that you are willing to pay, or bear, whatever the cost may be in order to let the person who has sinned against you go free. Whom do you pay? The question is foolish. It's not a person or being that requires the payment. The circumstance and situation requires payment. For you to let the violator off the hook, you have to relinquish the right to restitution, which means you simply bear the loss. In every case of forgiveness, it is the violated who suffers, not the violator.

Remember too that every occurrence of forgiveness is also an act of substitution. It is actually the only legally acceptable form of substitution. But for it to be legal the only one who can do it is the violated, and they must embrace it voluntarily, willingly, for it will cost them. But it is acceptable for them to drop the charges if they should see fit and are willing to pay the price of doing so. And this, too, dear friend, is what was transpiring at Calvary. God was not receiving restitution; He was giving us forgiveness. The God of this universe, the God we have violated, willingly suffered so we can go free. This is why Jesus said, "The creditor frankly forgave them both."

When this realization came home to my Muslim friend, you could see the lights turning on. You could see the wheels turning. He looked back at me with utter shock and asked, "Are you telling me that Jesus was God? Was Jesus the God that I've sinned against? Was God willing to bear my sin so that I could go free?"

"'Flesh and blood has not revealed this unto you,'" I said simply.

His quiet eyes met mine. "How I wish that as a Muslim I had a God who would do that for me. . . . Oh, how I wish I had a Savior like that!"

"You do!" I assured him. "Jesus is not only the Savior of the Christians; He is the Savior of the world—especially those who believe! And that includes Muslims too!"

"I don't know if I could ever call myself a Christian," he replied, "considering how Christians have treated us Muslims. But I do want this type of god."

We knelt right there, and he accepted God, in the person of Jesus Christ, as his Savior and Lord. Whether or not my friend will ever call himself a Christian, God knows his heart. He may be the only Muslim I've ever known who worshipped Jesus Christ as his God, Lord, and Savior.

Jesus never considered Himself to be a third party, separate from the relationship between God and us. He and His Father were one. They were the violated party. They were connected so closely that in looking at Jesus, one could perceive the Father. Why? Because it was the Father indwelling His Son, Jesus. The words Jesus spoke, the works Jesus performed, were not only Jesus' deeds but His Father's as well. The Father, according to Jesus, was living in Him, doing His work. Jesus was left at the Temple in

Jerusalem for three days at the age of 12, lost at the close of the Passover celebration. Upon finding Him, Mary and Joseph, after scolding Him, received this question from Jesus: "And he said unto them, How is it that ye sought me? wist ye not that I must be about my Father's business?" (Luke 2:49, KJV).

Did this principle apply to everything Jesus did? The biblical answer is yes. Jesus was the exact representation of the Father in all things. Was the Father still dwelling in His Son on the cross? In looking at Jesus on the cross, are we seeing the Father? If answered correctly, the answer to this question can open new and living perceptions of God's character. Can we still see the Father in His Son, even when suspended between heaven and earth between two thieves? The answer is yes!

Look at the words of Paul the apostle. When referring to the cross, Paul stated, "God was in Christ reconciling the world to Himself, not counting their trespasses against them" (2 Cor. 5:19). Where was the Father? In Christ! This has serious implications. Did not Jesus cry out that His Father had forsaken Him? Yes, but did the Father really forsake His Son, or did Jesus simply feel as if His Father had forsaken Him? The words of the prophet Isaiah are pertinent here. "But your iniquities have made a separation between you and your God, and your sins have hidden His face from you so that He does not hear" (Isa. 59:2).

Isaiah did not say that God separates from us when we sin, but rather that our sin separates us. How? Sin, once again, produces in our conscience the psychological and emotional dynamic of guilt, shame, and condemnation—psychological torment. Once a person is under the weight of condemnation, he/she can easily begin to believe that God is against him/her, too, supposing that God is the source of these feelings of condemnation. Sin begins to paint a perception of God that is untrue. Sin, via guilt and shame, begins to hide God's reconciling face from us and makes us feel as if God is now harboring ill feelings toward us. Just like the woman caught in adultery, the last thing we expect to hear from God is "I do not condemn you" (John 8:11).

Jesus, on Calvary, was personally encountering the same psychological reaction to our sin that sin produces in us. Did He feel as if God were far away? Absolutely! Doesn't sin make you feel that way? But we must believe that God is closest when we feel as if He is the furthest away, because that is when we need Him the most.

Although not perceived by Jesus on the cross, the Father was still "in

Christ" doing "His work." This paints a completely different picture of the Father's position at Calvary. During a series of presentations in Montana I made the announcement that on the following night we would be covering the subject of God's love as revealed through the sufferings of Jesus on the cross. Afterward a woman approached me and informed me that she would not be coming tomorrow night, but would be back the following evening. When I pressed her for a reason, she exclaimed, "The subject of the cross scares me. Everyone says we see God's love there. I've never seen anything but His anger." My heart went out to this woman as I began to understand what many feel when contemplating Calvary. Yes, they fall in love with Jesus because He was willing to take the Father's wrath in our place, but this way of viewing Calvary does nothing to enlighten us in regard to the character of the Father. On the contrary, it damages it. We fall in love with Jesus, but are still afraid of God. "What would God the Father have done to us if Jesus had not stepped forward? I'm sure thankful Jesus was willing to face Him so I don't have to." When we paint Calvary in these terms, we paint God as saying, "I don't care who suffers, innocent or guilty—somebody just better."

We must not say that the Father punished Jesus on the cross, either. To say this denies the basic truth that Jesus and His Father are one. We must also never say that Jesus persuaded the Father to forgive at the cross. Once again, this would separate their oneness. The purpose of the cross was not to persuade the Father to forgive us, but to reveal the forgiveness that was already there. The cross was not the means of God's forgiveness, but the very act of forgiveness itself. The Father did not punish Jesus for our sins at Calvary, nor did Jesus pay God back for our sins. God was *in* Christ! The role the Father played at Calvary was not the punisher but the punished! He was in His Son on the cross.

What caused the punishment of God on Calvary? Think about it in different terms. What ended Jesus' life? Think back to our previous chapters. What is the enemy here? What do we need to fear above all else? It's not God, but sin! Our sin caused Christ excruciating psychological torment and caused the sensation of separation from His Father.

I will admit that it's easier to put the cause of Jesus' suffering on God rather than on our sin, because we don't want to be the ones who are responsible for what Christ endured. But we must not yield to this temptation. Isaiah gives us insight into our reluctance to become responsible for Jesus's suffering, but our resistance has caused Calvary to produce decimation of God's character rather than its enlightenment.

"He was despised and forsaken *of men*, a man of sorrows and acquainted with grief; and like one from whom men hide their face He was despised, and we did not esteem Him. Surely our griefs He Himself bore, and our sorrows He carried; yet we ourselves esteemed Him stricken, smitten of God, and afflicted" (Isa. 53:3, 4). "But he was wounded *because of our transgressions*, he was crushed *because of our iniquities*: the chastisement of our welfare was upon him, and with his stripes *we were healed*" (verse 5, MT).

This misunderstanding of Calvary is precisely why this dear sister in Montana could not possibly see God's love at the cross. She could see Jesus' love, but not God's. She had separated God and Jesus and thus seen God as the punisher. Yet when she began to see that God was "in Christ" and that it was our sins that had caused the great suffering Christ endured, then her heart, for the first time, was liberated to begin perceiving how much the Father truly loved her.

We must not make a distinction between Jesus and the Father at Calvary, or the picture of the Father becomes pretty dark. If we don't yield to the temptation to separate Them, but rather make our sin the source of Jesus' suffering, then we immediately begin to see the self–abandoning nature of a heroic God who would risk all of heaven—even His own existence—in order to save us from our sin.

Jesus came to save us not from an angry God, but "from our sins." Again, we do not need to be afraid of God; we need to be afraid of sin! We do not need to be saved from God; we need to be saved from sin. God and Jesus are one. God did not punish Jesus, nor did Jesus persuade the Father to forgive. Jesus was no third party! Jesus was God incarnate. The violated party willingly and voluntarily bore the loss Himself so that the violators could go free. In one word, Calvary was a divine act of forgiveness. Paul states this in two verses.

"Namely, that God was in Christ reconciling the world to Himself, not counting their trespasses against them, and He has committed to us the word of reconciliation" (2 Cor. 5:19).

God was in His Son, not counting our trespasses against us. In other words, He was forgiving. Calvary was as if God were saying to the entire world, "Charges have been dropped." But aren't there conditions? Yes, but the conditions of forgiveness are always paid by the Forgiver, not the forgiven. Remember, it cost the two debtors nothing to be forgiven, but it cost the forgiver something to forgive. God has forgiven the world, for He bore the sins of the world. Let's look at Paul again.

"Be kind to one another, tender-hearted, forgiving each other, just as God in Christ also has forgiven you" (Eph. 4:32).

Paul is clear! He saw the Father's role at Calvary not as the punisher but as the punished. Far from the Father being persuaded by Christ to forgive humanity, he saw the Father as being in Christ engaged in the act of forgiving humanity. Calvary is not the means by which God can forgive; Calvary is the very act of divine forgiveness itself.

Forgiveness is the violated party willingly and voluntarily putting themselves in the place of the violator. The violated bears the loss that the violator inflicted so that the violator can go free. This is Calvary!

Yet to say that God has forgiven the entire world raises some questions. Where is the need for repentance, confession, and faith? If God has forgiven the world, does that mean that all will be saved at last? To answer these questions, we turn our attention to the next chapter.

Chapter Thirteen

Charizomai

"God is not a man; He does not cherish enmity, nor harbor a feeling of revenge. It is not because God has an angry feeling in His heart against a sinner that he asks forgiveness, but because the sinner has something in his heart. God is all right, the man is all wrong; therefore God forgives the man, that he also may be all right."—E. J. WAGGONER.

"We do not repent in order to convince God to forgive."—STANLEY MONTWELL.

If understanding God's role in our suffering is the greatest misunderstood concept of God's goodness today, His forgiveness is a close second.

There are many misconceptions about our God and His forgiveness, and I believe they revolve around chronology. Let me explain.

In Paul's letter to the Romans, he asked, "Or do you think lightly of the riches of His kindness and tolerance and patience, not knowing that the kindness of God leads you to repentance?" (Rom. 2:4).

Please notice what takes place first in this verse. It's God's goodness that is the cause of our repentance. It is alarming to me that many today don't view it like this.

When we sin, we immediately begin to encounter a sense of guilt and condemnation. Under this weight, many go one step further and begin to feel as if God is also condemning them. Have you ever wrestled with feeling condemned by God? So have I. How do we normally respond to these feelings? We don't want to be lost in the end, so we get on our knees and begin to repent! Yet, pay attention to our motive. We feel as if God is against us. His goodness is now suspended until we confess and repent. So we begin to pray, "God, if You'll forgive me just this once, I promise I will never do that again!" And we mean it, but the reason we are doing this concerns me. We feel as if God's kindness is now being withheld and that we must repent in order to reinstate it. If our feelings are true, then God's kindness does not lead us to repentance—but our repentance leads to God's kindness!

This is in direct contradiction to the Bible's teaching in regard to God's kindness. Where did we get this idea? I believe it is a misunderstanding of other verses, such as the following from John.

"If we confess our sins, He is faithful and righteous to forgive us our sins and to cleanse us from all unrighteousness" (1 John 1:9).

Most of us read this verse when we are under the weight of feeling as if God is condemning us. Remember that God condemns sin, not the sinner. God convicts the sinner, and many of us interpret this as His condemnation. We read this verse and immediately set about inducing God to let go of His ill feelings toward us, through confessing, repenting, and sometimes even greater means of penance.

I am alarmed by our degradation of His character when we feel as if we need to convince or persuade Him to forgive. Yet . . . doesn't the verse say that He will forgive only "if" we do something first? It all depends on how you define the word "forgive." We most often define it as "God letting go of negative feelings He has toward us over what we have done." But is this correct? Is this the biblical understanding of God's forgiveness, or could we be wrong?

Isaiah makes an interesting statement: "But your iniquities have made a separation between you and your God, and your sins have hidden His face from you so that He does not hear" (Isa. 59:2). Many of us read this verse and assume that when we sin, God either takes a step back from us or He hides His face from us. But this verse is not talking about what God does when we sin. This verse is talking about what sin does to us when we sin. Sin causes guilt and shame, a sense of condemnation. It makes us feel as if God is far away when in reality He is not! It is when we feel as if He is the furthest away that He is the closest. Yet we feel as if He is far away, our "conscience bearing witness," our own "thoughts alternately accusing or else defending" us (Rom. 2:15). Just like David after he had cut off a piece of Saul's robe, our conscience is bothering, or "smiting," us! (1 Sam. 24:5).

But this is going on inside of *us*, not God! Biblical forgiveness refers to a change in *us*, not God. I would like to teach you a little Greek and Hebrew. There are at least five different words in the original languages of the Bible to explain forgiveness: *nasa, salach, aphiemi, apoluo,* and *charizomai.*

VIOLATION

Violator	Violated
shame and guilt	ill feelings toward violator
nasa (Hebrew), salach (Hebrew), aphemi (Greek), apoluo (Greek)	charizomai (Greek)
English: forgiveness	English: forgiveness
a removal of guilt and shame from the psyche of the violator	a letting go of ill feelings toward the violator transpiring within the violated
accomplished through repentance, confession, and faith	when used in relation to God, has already transpired for the world (see chapter 12)

As I explained previously, in any violation there is a violator and a violated. Therefore, you have two separate and distinct psychological and emotional dynamics taking place simultaneously. You have, in any given situation, that which is taking place in the heart of the violated, and that which is taking place in the psyche of the violator. Let's look first at what is taking place in the violator.

Have you ever done something you know you shouldn't have? Of course. What do you begin to feel afterward? Guilt, shame, sense of condemnation, psychological and emotional torment.

This and more is transpiring in the heart of the violator. Even if this person is not experiencing these now, a day is coming when all consciences will be quickened and the guilt and shame of sin will come crashing down on the hearts and minds of those who have ever committed a violation or transgression. Under this soul-crushing guilt their lives, if left to bear it alone, will be crushed out.

We need to look at how God frees us from this soul-crushing guilt. Remember, God's forgiveness is what sets us free in order to look into the eyes of God again and not be destroyed. David gives us some insight into this idea.

"For You, Lord, are good, and ready to forgive, and abundant in lovingkindness to all who call upon You" (Ps. 86:5).

The tragedy of this verse is that many have thought that it refers to the aspect of forgiveness that transpires in the violated's heart. When we violate the laws of peace and happiness, the guilt and shame of our sin causes us to feel as if God is condemning us. These feelings paint for us an incorrect picture of God, and this picture can be very hard to erase. And so we read the above verse and immediately interpret it as telling us that God is "ready to forgive" and will let go of all the ill feelings of condemnation that He is feeling toward us if we will just do something first.

Wouldn't the good and "abundantly lovingkind" thing be not to harbor these things toward us in the first place? It doesn't seem "abundant" to hold something against someone until that person apologizes first! And we set about to repent, confess, beg, and promise in order to convince our God, who is already "ready," to now become more than "willing" and actually do it.

This misperception greatly damages our understanding of God's love. What's worse, this verse is addressing something entirely different. The word "forgiveness" in this verse is translated from the Hebrew word *salach*. It is related to *nasa*, which refers to the removal of the guilt and condemnation produced by sin in the psyche of the violator, not to the removal of ill feelings in the heart of the violated. It's referring, not to any change taking place in the violated, but rather, a change occuring in the violator.

Isaiah writes, "Let the wicked forsake his way and the unrighteous man his thoughts; and let him return to the Lord, and He will have compassion on him, and to our God, for He will abundantly pardon" (Isa. 55:7). We may think this verse is saying that if we will forsake our sin and turn to God, He will let go of our sin and not hold it against us anymore, but that's not what it is saying at all.

This verse is not referring to a change taking place on God's side of the violation (the violated). If it were, this would be a very dark picture of our God, who would be saying, "I will let it go if you get your act together." The misapplication of this verse has led many into a very behaviorally focused religion. The word "pardon" in this verse is taken from the Hebrew word *salach*, which refers to bringing about a very different experience in the psyche of the violator, to take away the individual's guilt and shame.

Another Old Testament prophet, Nehemiah, shares, "They refused to obey, and they were not mindful of Your wonders that You did among them. But they hardened their necks, and in their rebellion they appointed a leader to return to their bondage. But You are God, ready to pardon, gracious and merciful, slow to anger, abundant in kindness, and did not forsake them" (Neh. 9:17. NKJV). Again, the word "pardon" comes from *salach* and implies that with our cooperation, God is ready to cleanse our conscience.

This does not imply that God is willing to cleanse only if we make the first move. God makes the first move! God's readiness is an active readiness where He is taking the first steps in trying to induce us to cooperate. Why do we need to cooperate? Because *salach* is about bringing about a change in the psyche of the *violator*. If the violator denies having done anything wrong, then God can't possibly lead the individual through confession and repentance to a new, clean conscience. If the violator refuses to believe in God's prevenient forgiveness (I'll explain what this is in a moment), then God can't bring that person to a sense of assurance. God is longing and actively pursuing us! He is ready and motivated to bring about in us a sense of peace and acceptance in the place of our guilt and shame, if we will just cooperate with Him and let Him do it.

This is what John was referring to when He wrote, "If we confess our sins, He is faithful and righteous to forgive us our sins and to cleanse us from all unrighteousness" (1 John 1:9). This verse does not say that if we confess, God will let it go as if it never happened, and then cleanse His heart from all the ill feelings He had harbored toward us. Not at all! The verse says that the cleansing takes place in *us!* He will forgive us of that sin and cleanse us from its accompanying guilt and shame!

In 1 John 1:9 the English word "forgive" comes from the Greek word *aphiemi*, referring to the removal of guilt from the violator's own psyche. It is related to the Greek word *apoluo*, which carries a similar meaning.

Now let's look at one final word for forgiveness from the Bible's original languages. The word is *charizomai*, and it makes all the difference in the world. Unlike the previous words we've examined, this word *does* refer to the violated letting go of ill feelings that person may be harboring in his or her heart toward the violator.

In his second letter to the church in Corinth, Paul wrote, "So that on the contrary you should rather forgive and comfort him, otherwise such a one might be overwhelmed by excessive sorrow. . . . But one whom you forgive anything, I forgive also; for indeed what I have forgiven, if I have forgiven anything, I did it for your sakes in the presence of Christ" (2 Cor. 2:7). For in what respect were you treated as inferior to the rest of the churches, except that I myself did not become a burden to you? Forgive me this wrong!" (2 Cor. 12:13). Paul uses *charizomai* numerous times, and all these refer to the violated, in his or her own heart, letting the violator off the hook.

We see that the word "forgiveness" can refer to two separate but related things. First, it can be the act of cleansing the violator from guilt and shame. Second, it can refer to the violated, in his or her heart, releasing the violator, letting that person off the hook in spite of what he or she has done. Paul states that we are to *charizomai* and then seek to "comfort him." Here we see that Paul understood the dual aspects of forgiveness. Paul is admonishing his readers to *charizomai* (let it go) and then seek to "comfort him" (cleanse the violator of feelings of guilt and shame).

Now let's look at *charizomai* in relation to God and us. Remember, when referring to cleansing the conscience of the violator in relation to God and ourselves, forgiveness always appears in the future tense, waiting for the cooperation of the violator. But with *charizomai* in the picture, there is a dramatic change from the future tense to the past.

"Be kind to one another, tender-hearted, forgiving each other, just as God in Christ also has forgiven you" (Eph. 4:32).

Paul is referring to Calvary, where, as we discovered in the last chapter, God had forgiven the world. By using the Greek word *charizomai,* Paul is saying that God has already "let us off the hook" in His heart, and we are to do the same for others.

But what about repentance, confession, and faith? This is the amazing truth of the gospel. Remember that repentance, confession, and faith are the means whereby God brings about change in us, and they were never meant as a means of bringing about a change in God. Calvary reveals that God in His heart has forgiven this world, whether its inhabitants have or ever will repent or not. Calvary was not the means whereby God could forgive, but was rather a manifestation of the forgiveness already present in His heart.

Would we be justified in withholding forgiveness from those who had wronged us until they says they're sorry? We may not be justified, but we do it. And then when they says they're sorry, we ask if they're really sorry, expecting him to promise never to do it again. We make the mistake that God is altogether like us. This is why we tell God in our prayers for forgiveness that we are *really* sorry and promise never to do it again. But this is not repentance or confession. It's a form of begging God to "let it go," to forgive. We need to back up and reason this out.

If we are not justified in withholding forgiveness from others until they apologize because we are admonished to forgive as God forgives, then God cannot be the type of person who would withhold forgiveness until we apologize. His forgiveness is much larger than what we typically perceive. He, *in His heart,* has forgiven us even before we have repented.

Yet there is more in Scripture regarding how things transpire in God's heart in relation to our sins.

Paul writes to the Colossians, "When you were dead in your transgressions and the uncircumcision of your flesh, He made you alive together with Him, having forgiven us all our transgressions" (Col. 2:13).

The word "forgiven" once again comes from *charizomai.* And notice how many of their sins Paul stated that God had, in His heart, forgiven and when. Paul does not make this statement after the Colossian believers had repented, confessed, got their act together, or even said a sinner's prayer. Rather, it was while they were dead in their transgressions. God made us alive together with Christ, forgiving all our transgressions. Notice how many—all! What if they hadn't confessed them yet? What if they hadn't repented of them? What if they haven't believed yet? What if they hadn't even committed the sins yet? Paul chose the word *charizomai* specifically, and therefore meant exactly what he was writing: God, in His heart, has already "forgiven," or "let go," of all sins for all people.

You ask, "Then how can anyone be lost?" Salvation, contrary to popular Christianity, is not convincing God to forgive our sin, but rather accepting His prevenient forgiveness[1] so that we can experience cleansing from our guilt and shame. Then, on the day of revelation, we will not have our lives crushed out by the psychological and emotional torment of our sin. People can be lost even if God loves and forgives them, if they never believe they are loved and forgiven. It's not arbitrary; it's inherent. It's cause and effect.

Glory $\longrightarrow$ **Sin** $\longrightarrow$ **Torment/Wrath** $\longrightarrow$ **Death**

(Through repentance, faith, and confession)

Glory $\longrightarrow$ **Forgiveness** $\longrightarrow$ **Peace** $\longrightarrow$ **Life Everlasting**

Through forgiveness, God is restoring us to be able to live in His presence once again.

Do you remember the story of the woman in the Bible who was caught in adultery? Here was a woman who had been raised in Old Testament culture. She understood the consequences of her actions. After she was caught, what do you think was transpiring in her heart and mind during the sequence of those events? Maybe shame, guilt, fear, and a sense of condemnation? How do you think she perceived God to be thinking and feeling toward her at that moment? Have you ever felt condemned by God? We are so quick to forget that God condemns sin but not the sinner. God hates sin with a hatred as strong as death, *but* He loves the sinner with a love that is stronger than death! Yet here was this woman surrounded by feelings of condemnation, and she was feeling condemned especially by God. Although this was in her head, it was not what God was feeling.

How many times do we make this mistake? When we are under a weight of condemnation, we transpose what's going on inside of us onto God and assume that the same thing is happening in Him toward us. The apostle John sought to help us escape from this wrong picture of God when he penned the words, "If our heart condemns us, God is greater than our heart, and knows all things" (1 John 3:20, NKJV). When we feel condemned, God is much larger than that. He's not condemning us. How do we know? Look at the very first words He shared with the woman who thought God was condemning her for her adulterous acts. Here was God Himself, and before anything else was said to this woman, God looked into her eyes and said, "Neither do I condemn you" (John 8:11, NKJV). In other words, *"I don't condemn you . . ."* Wow! Could this really be true?

Many people mistakenly see justification as something that happens in God. They think it refers to a decision that God makes about you. But look at condemnation, the opposite of justification. Condemnation is produced by sin in our conscience. Condemnation is the guilt and shame we feel inside as a result of being out of harmony with what we know to be right. As the opposite of condemnation, justification is the psychological and emotional reality of peace we feel inside when we truly believe we have been forgiven. Justification is not a decision God makes about us. Rather, it is a psychological change that God brings about in us, in our own psyche, our conscience, when we allow Him to take away those feelings of condemnation and guilt and replace them with the perfect peace of knowing we have been forgiven. This peace changes our entire life.

Does this mean we should not ask God to forgive us? Absolutely not! But we need to ask intelligently. We are not to ask God to do something He has already done. So understand that when you are asking God to forgive you, you are not asking Him to let it go, but rather to set you free from the guilt and shame you are currently under because of your sin. You are to believe that God in His heart has already forgiven you, and, based on that, to ask Him to give you the psychological and emotional peace, instead of guilt, that only He can provide. When you ask God for forgiveness, you are asking Him to enable you to experience that forgiveness subjectively in your own heart and mind.

The probability of your sinning again before the Lord comes back is pretty high. And the next time it happens, you are going to have to choose to picture God in one of two ways.

Here is the first option. Having sinned, you will be plagued once again by guilt and shame, your heart and conscience will begin painting a picture of a God who is now against you, and you will feel that you need to return to a position of favor with Him. So you get on your knees and begin to beg and plead through "repentance" and "confession" to convince God to let it go and to reinstate you into His favor. You may even make such promises as, "Lord, if You will forgive me just this once, I promise I will never do that again." But for those of you who have taken this route before, tell me what inevitably happens. Having promised God that you wouldn't, you accidentally do. And now how do you feel in relation to the first offense? You feel even worse, and so you get back on your knees asking Him again, promising again, "God, I'm sorry, but if You will give me just one more try—I really mean it, Lord—it will never happen again." But as most have experienced, it does happen again! And now you feel even worse than the first two times. And so you get back on your knees, and the cycle never seems to end. Do you know the end result of having this picture of God? One morning you wake up, having sinned too many times after promising Him you wouldn't, and you just don't think you have the strength to convince Him to forgive you one more time. Do you know what you do? You chuck the whole thing and quit trying! "There is a way that seems right to a person, but its end is the way to death" (Prov. 14:12, NRSV).

Or you can choose the second option: The next time you sin, you can, rather than depending on your feelings, fight the fight of faith. Choose to believe that no matter how you feel, God is not condemning you, but is still madly in love with you and wants to save you from the relationally damaging effects of what you have done. Let me share with you a true story that helps illustrate what I'm trying to say.

There once was a beautiful Latin young woman named Maria, who lived in Brazil. Not only was she drop-dead gorgeous; she was also beautiful where it counts, on the inside. At school during recess the students would play soccer, and when it was Maria's turn to be a team captain, she would start not with the most talented soccer player but with the worst one. Why? Because she knew what it felt like to be picked last at recess. As she grew up, she began getting the best grades in her class and showed real academic talent. On top of all this, she had a sparkly sense of humor, which gave her the ability to bring a smile to the grumpiest person's face.

Maria had a dream that one day she would take all these talents and gifts, leave her small village, and go to the city of Rio de Janeiro to make a success out of her life. But her mother feared that day, for her mother knew that if Maria ever went to that city, there was only one way that Maria could support herself.

Then it happened. One morning, after Maria had grown much older, her mother went into Maria's bedroom to find her worst nightmare had begun. Maria's bed lay empty, with only a note explaining where she had gone. Her mother scrounged up all the money she had and bought a bus ticket. Then, with some leftover coins, she stopped by one of those self-service photo booths and took picture after picture of herself. Then she got on the bus and went to the city.

She went to houses of prostitution, casinos, crack houses, hourly hotels, anywhere she thought Maria might pass by. At each place she would write a message on the back of a picture and then tape it to a pay phone, staple it to a bulletin board, or stick it in the cracks of a bathroom mirror. Three weeks went by, and finally the pictures were all gone. Her mother had nothing left to do but get back on the bus and go home to wait.

After six months crept by, it happened. Maria woke up one morning in one of those institutions. Wanting to leave before her partner for that night awoke, she grabbed what little clothes she had and made her way down a cigarette smoke-filled hallway. The innocence on her face was gone, replaced by a vacant expression of loss and hopelessness. Pain marked her every gesture. Upon reaching the lobby, she remembered that she needed to make a phone call. As she picked up the receiver from the nearest pay phone, there was a picture of her mother, miraculously still there.

At first she didn't recognize who it was, but then it dawned on her. It was her mom! She dropped the phone and picked up the picture, wondering what a picture of her mom was doing in a place like this. Then she flipped over the picture to find these words written by her mother.

"My dearest Maria, whatever you have done, whatever you've become, it doesn't matter to me. Just come home. I love you. Your mommy."

Tears began to fill Maria's eyes. She clutched the picture close to her chest. She packed up what little she had left, and she went home.

But what I would like to ask is Why didn't Maria go home sooner? What did Maria expect to get from her mother if she went home and told her that she was a prostitute? Rejection? Condemnation? Disapproval? Unbelief? Anger? Not wanting to face any of these, she remained far, far away. But when Maria discovered that her mother already knew, and that before she had repented or confessed her mother had already forgiven her, loved her, and was inviting her back home, then and only then did she pack her things and go home.

And so I ask you, "What is your picture of God?" Is it one of a God whom you need to convince to forgive you, or is it the picture of a God who already has and is saying to you, "I don't condemn you. Whatever you've done, whatever you've become, My child, just come home."[2] In only one of these pictures is an eternal salvation waiting to guide us home. Do you want to experience this forgiveness? In the next chapter I'll show you how. Will you choose at this moment to believe that He has already forgiven you? If you will, your life will never be the same.

---

[1] Prevenient refers to those things God does for us before we repent, confess, or believe.

[2] "She said, 'No one, Lord.' And Jesus said, 'I do not condemn you, either. Go. From now on sin no more'" (John 8:11).

Chapter Fourteen

The Awakening

"Power is of two kinds. One is obtained by the fear of punishment and the other by acts of love. Power based on love is a thousand times more effective and permanent than the one derived from fear of punishment."—MAHATMA GANDHI.

"Only by love is love awakened."—ELLEN. G. WHITE.

"God saves by persuasion, not compulsion, for compulsion is no attribute of God."—EPISTLE TO DIOGNETUS.

"Believe not God is in your heart, child, but rather, you're in the heart of God."—UNKNOWN.

Have you ever honestly been challenged by the story of Calvary and wondered what it was all really about? I find myself constantly re-evaluating my understanding of God's great sacrifice to save me, only to have my heart strangely moved each time. I am ever finding love for Him awakened more deeply, as I am brought to some deeper realization of what God, in His infinite love, was willing to do for me.

The statements that God made leading up to that Friday afternoon are puzzling. Scripture indicates clearly that Jesus understood that He was going to die and be raised again in three days.[1] Throughout His life Jesus saw Himself victorious in the end. He responded to the religious rulers of His day by saying, "Destroy this temple and in three days I will raise it up!" (John 2:19). On His way to Jerusalem just before His final week on earth, He assured His disciples about His resurrection.[2]

Just before His death Jesus shared, "No one can kill me without my consent—I lay down my life voluntarily. For I have the right and power to lay it down when I want to and also the power to take it again. For My

Father has given Me this right" (John 10:18, TLB). The *New Jerusalem Bible* translates His words this way: "I lay it down of my own free will, and as I have power to lay it down, so I have power to take it up again; and this is the command I have received from my Father." On the cross He told the thief beside Him, "you shall be *with Me* in Paradise" (Luke 23:43).

Nonetheless, even with each of these statements, Jesus' belief that He was going to rise again on the third day was just that—a belief. This revelation was "given" to Him from God the Father. Jesus took this belief with Him all the way to Calvary. It was this belief in His own resurrection that led Him to impart, even to the thief beside Him, the sense of forgiveness and the assurance that he would end up with Him in Paradise. Yet in order to understand fully what Jesus endured on the cross, it must be understood that Jesus' interaction with the thief took place sometime during the *first* three hours of Calvary.

Jesus was on the cross for six hours, not just three. The first three hours are recorded for us in detail. This, I believe, is primarily because His suffering during that time was mostly external, in His physical person, easily noticeable and recordable by His disciples. But during the last three hours Jesus' suffering transitioned to internal, psychological, and emotional. His disciples could not perceive during those last three hours what was happening inside of Him. They could not say, "Well, this is what He is feeling right now." So instead Scripture simply becomes strangely silent.

Other prophetic passages reveal, though, that His mental and emotional suffering during these last three hours became so intense that they almost eclipsed the things He was suffering physically. Jesus entered into dark mental, psychological, and emotional suffering. Having taken upon Himself the responsibility for our sins, His mind and heart began to be tormented by the guilt and shame of the sins of this world. Imagine for a moment what life would be like for you if you had the cognizant realization of every rape, murder, and child molestation happening as you read this sentence. Forget feeling responsible. What would it be like simply to be perfectly and keenly aware of it all? Now consider that Jesus not only was intensely aware of every sin that has taken place from the beginning of time until its end, but also took full responsibility for them!

In the midst of Jesus' awareness and feeling of responsibility, I believe Satan was present. Satan took his opportunity and engaged in an effort to break God's will and force Him to let go of His hold on the human race. Satan pressed close to the heart of Jesus, and whispered, "You don't understand, Jesus. Sin is so offensive to a holy God, God hates sin so much, that this is going to separate You from Your Father *forever*. Did you hear that, Jesus? *Forever!*"

Before we go any further, we need to look at where this is revealed in Scripture. I would like you to look at the little-noticed passage of Psalm 88.

"I am reckoned among those who go down to the pit;[3] I have become like a man without strength, forsaken among the dead,[4] like the slain who lie in the grave, whom You remember no more. . . . Selah" (Ps. 88:4-7).

Take note of the statement ". . . like the slain who lie in the grave, whom You remember no more." There is a death that all die (unless the Lord returns first), lost and saved alike. Righteous or wicked, saint or sinner, believer or unbeliever, all experience this death. And likewise all will be remembered in the sense that they will be resurrected. Everyone. Paul stated, "For as in Adam all die, so also in Christ *all* will be made alive" (1 Cor. 15:22). Jesus said, "Do not marvel at this; for an hour is coming, in which all who are in the tombs will hear His voice, and will come forth; those who did the good deeds to a resurrection of life, those who committed the evil deeds to a resurrection of judgment" (John 5:28, 29).

But there is a death to which the Bible refers as the "second death,"[5] which the lost will experience. In the second death there is no hope of being "remembered" again, because there is no hope of resurrection. Certainly God will always lovingly remember those who refuse to spend eternity with Him, but in the sense of being "remembered" for the purpose of resurrection, they will be forgotten.

Now, I want to be careful. Christians believe that Jesus was resurrected. Although they also believe that the Father did not forsake His Son on the cross, that doesn't mean that Jesus did not feel as if He had been forsaken. Likewise, even though Jesus would be resurrected three days later, the question we must answer is During those final three hours, did He *feel* as if He would be resurrected?

You see, by the sixth hour of Calvary, Jesus' mind had been tormented for three hours with the guilt and shame of our sins. Add to this the whisperings of Satan. How did all this truly affect Him? We cannot know that fully yet. But what we do know is that this traumatic experience climaxed for Jesus with the cry "My God, My God, why have You forsaken Me?" (Matt. 27:46). By this point, feeling utterly forsaken of God, we have to ask ourselves, did Jesus *still* see Himself coming forth from the grave a conqueror? Could He see *through* the portals of the tomb? Certainly Jesus would later die with a reinstated sense of His Father's acceptance, but was this the case throughout His whole experience on the cross? Or is Psalm 88 revealing to us that Jesus went through a very dark time during which He thought—if even for a moment—that He was saying goodbye to life forever? I believe this to be exactly what Scripture is telling us.[6] Satan pressed hard against the mind and heart of Jesus, whispering that this separation between Him and His Father was to be *forever*.

And to make it worse, Satan's lies were, as they still are, mixed with a little bit of truth. God does hate sin with a hatred as strong as death. But what part was Satan purposely leaving out? He omitted the part about God loving the sinner with a love that is stronger than death! Satan purposely chose to focus only on God's attitude toward sin in hopes that Jesus would feel that this was His Father's attitude toward Himself as well. And it worked! Satan presented three things before Jesus: (1) all the glories of heaven; (2) the reuniting embrace of His Father; and (3) the adoration of the angels.

Up until this point on Calvary, Jesus' response could have been that He would save humanity and in three days have all these three blessings again. But not now! You see, now Jesus is feeling as if He is saying goodbye to life forever. And what is most painful to me, what brings tears to my eyes every time, is the thought that it was at this very moment that Satan compared all the adoration of the angels to how many times I, Herb Montgomery, would fail to give Him the adoration He deserves. I should have been there for Him, and I haven't been. I could have made His sacrifice easier, and I have not! I've spent a lifetime making Calvary harder for my Savior. And this touches deep, deep chords in my heart.

Yes, there was a time on the cross that Jesus held on to the hope that He could *both* save me and spend eternity in Paradise Himself, too. But as my sin pressed upon His heart and He began to *feel* forsaken of His Father, Satan's words closed in around Him. Jesus became encircled and alone. Satan began to echo, no, chant the two words that he had inspired all day. The rulers said them, the passersby said them, the Pharisees said them, even the soldiers and one of the thieves on the cross had said them: "Save Yourself!"[7] Over and over he whispered, "Save Yourself."

"In the same way the chief priests also, along with the scribes, were mocking Him among themselves and saying, 'He saved others; He cannot save Himself. Let this Christ, the King of Israel, now come down from the cross, so that we may see and believe!' Those who were crucified with Him were also insulting Him" (Mark 15:13, 32).

Satan and Jesus' accusers were dead right! He had lived His entire life in disinterested benevolence, saving others at every step. He had always put others before Himself. And now, once again, others must come first. What His assailants did not understand is that Jesus could have saved Himself. Never was His back against the wall. What He was enduring was voluntary, of His own volition, His own free will. But in order to save others, He must *not* now "save Himself"!⁸ Although He could save us, and He had the power to save Himself, He *could not* do both.

And this is what wins me to Him. He could have let me go. He could have chosen to save Himself rather than me. When Jesus was faced with eternal loss, knowing that He could either save Himself at an eternal and infinite loss to me, or He could save me at an eternal and infinite loss to Himself, love for me overwhelmed the heart of this God hanging upon a cross for me. His heart gripped tighter to me, He would not let me go, at any cost to Himself. He loves me! He screams out His heart cry for me, "I will save that young man at *any* cost to Myself." And He bowed His head and died.

Do you know why I am a Christian today, dear reader? It's not because I want to get to heaven or escape hell. The reason lies here at the cross. My God took into account all the glories of heaven, all the adoration of the angels, that reuniting embrace with His Father, and then looked at me. And seeing me in my lost condition, my God, from His heart, said, "heaven is not a place that I desire to be if he can't be there." *I* am what makes it Heaven for Him!

I have friends who ask, "What if there is no heaven, no hell, no reward, no punishment? What if all you are doing is for nothing?" And in the shadows of His great love for me, I very respectfully say, "I don't care! My God lived for me when there was no heaven in it for Him. And so, even if there is no heaven or hell, no reward or punishment, even if I get nothing out it, my God is so beautiful, so self-less, so self-abandoning, so giving and kind that I don't care if I don't live forever; it's not about me, it's all about Him! I have been loved by many, but never like this. I want Him to feel overloved and overjoyed. He is the most beautiful person I have ever encountered, and based on that alone He is worthy of my love every waking moment of my life. And whether it's realistic, whether it's possible or not, I will spend my eternity trying to outlove my God, because more than anyone else, He is the one who deserves someone trying, someone loving Him back the way He has loved me![9]

I would like to stop here and ask you to be honest. I stand in front of this kind of self-abandonment, this kind of love, and I am silenced. With tears in my eyes, my heart reaches away from my own self-centeredness, my own pursuits, and I reach out to a love like this. Is this really what God is like? God, do You really love me like this? Will You really love me regardless of the cost to Yourself? I feel the arguments rising: "Please, God, don't give up heaven for me; I'm not worth it." Yet I sense Him whispering, "I didn't do it because you were worthy. I did it because I love you . . . and you can't change that. Come, let Me enfold you in the love for which your heart has always longed." And I thank Him for His love for me.

Dear reader, after reading about God's great love for you, do you feel something as I do? What is it that you feel? Please take a moment and write down one-word descriptions of what you feel. Trust me on this.

Now look at your list.

Maybe you feel unworthy. Maybe you feel gratitude. Awe? Thankfulness? Forgiveness? Hope? Maybe just *wow!*

Let me ask you: Do you feel love? Do you feel God loving you? Do you feel love awakening in your heart in response to God?

If you do, what you're feeling is the awakening! It is the simultaneous miracle of loving while being loved. Remember, you were made for this. How did you lose it? Just like me, you believed lies about God. Jesus stated that He was going to restore to us the love for which we were made, through revealing the truth concerning what our God is truly like. He would reveal to us the truth, and the truth would set us free. This is what you have encountered today, my friend. You have just scratched the surface of what God intended your experience with Him to be like. Would you like what you feel to be a more consistent reality in your Christian experience? Would you like it to be more than just a passing moment in the pages of a book, a fleeting encounter that surfaces and then fades almost as quickly as it appeared?

This encounter did not result from a greater effort to get your behavior right, but from *seeing* more clearly what your heavenly Father is like. This must become our paramount passion, our focus, our emphasis. All else must be held as secondary to seeing and believing that God truly is the kind of person Jesus has revealed. God is love, and He loves you, dear reader. The more energy we consistently spend focusing on this, the more consistent will be our experience with Him. God is whispering, He's calling you to this experience. Will you put all aside and make knowing Him and His love for you your obsession?

"We know only a portion of the truth, and what we say about God is always incomplete. But when the Complete arrives, our incompletes will be canceled. When I was an infant at my mother's breast, I gurgled and cooed like any infant. When I grew up, I left those infant ways for good. We don't yet see things clearly. We're squinting in a fog, peering through a mist. But it won't be long before the weather clears and the sun shines bright! We'll see it all then, see it all as clearly as God sees us, knowing him directly just as he knows us! But for right now, until that completeness, we have three things to do to lead us toward that consummation: Trust steadily in God, hope unswervingly, love extravagantly. And the best of the three is love" (1 Cor. 13:9-13, Message).

---

[1] "For just as Jonah was three days and three nights in the belly of the sea monster, so will the Son of Man be three days and three nights in the heart of the earth" (Matt. 12:40). "This man stated, 'I am able to destroy the temple of God and to rebuild it in three days'"(Matt. 26:61). "Sir, we remember that when He was still alive that deceiver said, 'After three days I am to rise again'" (Matt. 27:63). "And He began to teach them that the Son of Man must suffer many things and be rejected by the elders and the chief priests and the scribes, and be killed, and after three days rise again" (Mark 8:31). "They will mock Him and spit on Him, and scourge Him and kill Him, and three days later He will rise again" (Mark 10:34).

[2] "For He was teaching His disciples and telling them, 'The Son of Man is to be delivered into the hands of men, and they will kill Him; and when He has been killed, He will rise three days later'" (Mark 9:31).

[3] "Therefore, I will allot Him a portion with the great, and He will divide the booty with the strong; because He poured out Himself to death, and was numbered with the transgressors; yet He Himself bore the sin of many, and interceded for the transgressors" (Isa. 53:12).

[4] "About the ninth hour Jesus cried out with a loud voice, saying, 'Eli, Eli, lama sabachthani?' that is, 'My God, my God, why have You forsaken Me?'" (Matt. 27:46).

[5] "Blessed and holy is the one who has a part in the first resurrection; over these the second death has no power, but they will be priests of God and of Christ and will reign with Him for a thousand years" (Rev. 20:6). "Then death and Hades were thrown into the lake of fire. This is the second death, the lake of fire" (verse 14). "But for the cowardly and unbelieving and abominable and murderers and immoral persons and all, liars, their part will be in the lake that burns with fire and brimstone, which is the second death" (Rev. 21:8).

[6] The argument in the past has been that since Jesus was resurrected, did He truly die the second death? But this is not the point at all. The point is: Which did He *feel* He was dying? And did those feelings, that He was saying goodbye to life forever, change the decision He would make? Is God truly other-centered, even when faced with the highest cost?

[7] "And saying, 'You who are going to destroy the temple and rebuild it in three days, save Yourself! If You are the Son of God, come down from the cross" (Matt. 27:40). "Save

Yourself, and come down from the cross!" (Mark 15:30). "If You are the King of the Jews, save Yourself!" (Luke 23:37). "One of the criminals who were hanged there was hurling abuse at Him, saying, 'Are You not the Christ? Save Yourself and us!'" (verse 39).

[8] "Or do you think that I cannot appeal to My Father, and He will at once put at My disposal more than twelve legions of angels?" (Matt. 26:53).

[9] This is what God is truly like. I hold up Calvary as the reason and answer for everything in my life. And if something contradicts what I see there, the type of person I see on the cross, then I must acquiesce that that picture is wrong. His primary purpose for going to Calvary: "Righteous Father, though the world does not know you, I know you. . . . I have made you known to them, and will continue to make you known in order that the love you have for me may be in them and that I myself may be in them" (John 17:25, 26, NIV).

Chapter Fifteen

By His Stripes

"Men never do evil so completely and cheerfully as when they do it from a religious conviction."—BLAISE PASCAL.

"Forgiveness is the fragrance the violet sheds on the heel that has crushed it." —MARK TWAIN.

Have you ever wondered why Jesus had to suffer such gross physical torment on the cross? Was His physical torment necessary to save humanity? Was it part of His mission to suffer such atrocities at the hands of human beings? It seems that He suffered as much hatred and violence as His human nature could endure! Why?

If the physical aspects of Jesus' sacrifice paid some part of a penalty, then the implications concerning the character of such a One who would demand such torture and torment are grave. The physical torment of crucifying criminals was the creation not of God, but of humanity. Nonetheless, the Bible is clear that God was overruling humanity's actions for a higher purpose. The Bible clearly states that it was part of Christ's mission to suffer as much hatred and violence at the hands of humans as His human nature could endure. It also says that it was necessary for Jesus to suffer physical torment in order to save humanity. But why? Read carefully the words of the apostle Peter.

"For truly in this city there were gathered together against Your holy servant Jesus, whom You anointed, both Herod and Pontius Pilate, along with the Gentiles and the peoples of Israel, to do whatever Your hand and Your purpose predestined to occur" (Acts 4:27, 28).

"This Man, delivered over by the predetermined plan and foreknowledge of God, you nailed to a cross by the hands of godless men and put Him to death" (Acts 2:23).

We must be clear. Jesus' physical sufferings played no role in paying some penalty for sin. What was their purpose? We need to be careful here, or the physical sufferings of Jesus won't illuminate our perceptions of God, but will further darken them. Humanity's captivity to sin is rooted and grounded in a misperception of God. Humanity's salvation, therefore, is rooted and grounded in an event that must reveal the truth about God and what He is like! Could Jesus' physical sufferings have been to reveal something that we otherwise would never have seen concerning God's heart toward us?

Notice what Jesus included in this "cup" that He said He *must* drink.

"So Jesus said to Peter, 'Put the sword into the sheath; the cup which the Father has given Me, shall I not drink it?'" (John 18:11).

It is interesting to note that Jesus was not referring to the psychological or emotional aspects of His sufferings. The cup that His Father had given Him to drink absolutely included the psychological and emotional aspects, but here we see that it also included His physical sufferings. Again, was it necessary for Jesus to suffer physically in order to save man? The answer seems to be yes. But be careful. In what sense? Isaiah says, "By His stripes [His physical suffering], *we are healed.*" (Isa. 53:5, NKJV). Healed of what? We are healed of our misperceptions of what we think God thinks and feels toward us. We have the wrong picture! And it is from this wrong picture that, through the events of the cross, God seeks to set us free.

Follow carefully the events of those hours leading up to and encompassing Jesus' infinite sacrifice for us and ponder the implications. What is this all saying about the God Jesus claimed to be and reveal? As we ponder, I believe that we will be healed of the destructive effects of the lies we have believed about our God. For it is by these events, understood correctly, that our hearts "are healed" and liberated to see the truth, to see the beauty of our God! He truly is beautiful if you can just *see* Him.

I also want you to consider how being freed from our misconceptions concerning Him will affect us. Jesus includes in the "cup" He must drink the sufferings that He is about to endure from this mob that is about to take Him away. But why? It was certainly not because the Father was demanding Jesus to be tormented! Remember, God was not outside His Son demanding payment, but *in* Him, "reconciling the world to Himself." (2 Cor. 5:19). Have you ever met someone who was extremely focused on self, extremely self-centered? What does it take to change this mind–set? What is necessary to reconcile that person to those about whom he or she couldn't care less? What does it take to turn that focus from self to others?

Usually it takes an incredible act of loving self-sacrifice from someone else on his or her behalf to awaken the realization that there are greater things in life to live for than self. If someone who is extremely self-centered can encounter this kind of love, then this love and only this love has the potential of changing their orientation from themselves to the One who loves them infinitely. Only by love is love awakened. "We love, because He first loved us" (1 John 4:19). God has one shot, and He must give all. He must make the revelation clear and compelling. It must be visible, historical, unforgettable. It must also be powerful enough to awaken in us deep sympathy and love for our God, transforming us at a heart level from living for ourselves to living for Him who died for us and rose again.* If this should fail, all is lost.

You see, it was our condition that made it necessary for Christ to suffer as much hatred and violence from our hands as His human nature could endure. Why? There is one theme that over and over screams out through Christ's suffering to our self-centered hearts. It is my prayer that this theme will be clearly perceived and believed in its lucid clarity as we let our hearts be moved in the pages ahead.

------

* "And He died for all, so that they who live might no longer live for themselves, but for Him who died and rose again on their behalf" (2 Cor. 5:15).

Chapter Sixteen

"He Frankly Forgave"

///

"Whatever I see the Father doing, I will do in like manner."
—JESUS *(see John 5:19)*

Let's consider, step by step, the closing events of Jesus' life, beginning with the events of His last evening with His disciples. What do we see there?

Jesus doubtless knew that there was one present who was feigning friendship in that upper room that night. Judas had been revealed to Jesus as the one who had chosen to betray Him. The events of that last supper in relation to Judas are truly shocking. Consider the act of foot washing in those days; they did not have indoor plumbing. Many church congregations still incorporate foot washing into their Communion service today. The church I attend does as well. It's an extraordinary experience to remind us that we are to take care of each other as brothers and sisters in Jesus. We are to focus on serving each other rather than on being served. Even in the light of each other's failures and defects, our fellow believers are to be the objects of our love and support, not our criticism. Foot washing is like saying to a brother or sister, "I've got your back."

So as Jesus was washing Judas' feet, you can imagine Judas thinking, *Well, maybe Jesus doesn't really know what I'm about to do.* But as they were eating, Jesus revealed to Judas that He had known the entire evening.

"Here at this table, sitting among us as a friend, is the man who will betray me" (Luke 22:21, NLT).

Notice what Jesus still called Judas—"a friend"! You can imagine the consternation Judas began to feel. *Why did he wash my feet?* he must have pondered.

As Judas is searching for the answer, Jesus' voice is heard as He takes the cup.

"This is My blood of the covenant, which is poured out for many for forgiveness of sins" (Matt. 26:28).[1]

Why was Jesus about to shed His blood? So we can experience the guilt-dismissing peace of forgiveness. As we have already discovered, one result of Jesus' death was that our consciences, our hearts, could be cleansed of the guilt and shame that plagues us because of our sin. We can be free from the guilt and shame that would otherwise one day crush out our life. Jesus held this cup so that we can go free.

Judas continued wrestling in his mind, *Well, He's offering it to them, but He couldn't possibly be offering it to me. I mean, I'm about to betray Him.*

"When He had taken a cup and given thanks, He gave it to them, saying, 'Drink from it, *all* of you.'" (verse 27).

Not 11 of you! Not just a few! But *all* of you! We are not told, but at whom do you think Jesus looked when He whispered "all of you"?

That's right. Judas.

Judas' heart trembled in the balance, *Me? But You don't know what I'm about to do. I'm about to betray You. Don't You understand? But wait, You said You do. Really? And You still forgive me? Are You really forgiving me?* Judas wrestled hard with the converting power of Jesus' love. But finally, pride hardened the heart of Judas. Pride overcame the desire to love Jesus back. And pushing back Jesus' extended gift of forgiveness, Judas, at that moment, slipped beyond the reach of mercy.

What do we see Jesus trying to communicate through these events? What can we learn about the God who is in Jesus, doing His work? What correction was Jesus seeking to make in our picture of God? In one word, Jesus was trying to teach Judas, and the world who would read the story for centuries to come, that God's primary feeling toward all of us is *forgiveness!* Could this be true? God's chief attribute is not stern justice lying in wait to punish us for our failures; God is a God whose chief feeling toward us is forgiveness.

It may seem too good to be true, but this is why believing the truth about God is called fighting the fight of faith. No matter what your feelings tell you, will you choose to believe that this is what God has always felt toward you every day of your life? The very first words we hear Jesus saying to us through the events of Calvary are "Whatever you've done, whatever you're about to do, I forgive you!"

What puzzles me is that when we fail, we never picture God being this understanding or forgiving. We view Him as a hard taskmaster who cuts us no slack—one screwup and that's it! Could it be that we've got it all wrong? He sees our own self-despising, and without censure He simply places His hands on our shoulders and encourages us to get back up. He simply says, "I know your spirit. I know your effort. I know you are trying. This is of greater value to Me than all the outward performance in the world *without heart*. I love you. I know your heart. I understand that at times the flesh is weak."

God loves you whether you sin or not. And this kind of love, this kind of understanding, although it could be taken for granted and abused, has the greatest potential to awaken the desire in us to live for this Being who loves us so unconditionally. Remember, He wants to change our focus from being self-centered to other-centered, and this can be awakened only by love and understanding.

Too often we have engaged in certain religious behaviors because we were afraid of what God would do to us if we didn't. But this is not at all what God wants. Remember, God is not the cause of our fear—*sin is!* It is our own self-centeredness that will hurt us. God loves us and is trying to awaken in us a conversion from being so focused on ourselves.

If your motive for serving God is fear of His punishment if you don't, it makes perfect sense to be concerned about such statements as "God loves you no matter how you live." It may appear that you are opening the door to live however you choose.

Yes, God loves you unconditionally. But that doesn't change the inherent destructiveness of sin. God may love you, but sin doesn't. Our motives for refraining from sin should not be fear of what God will do to us, but rather love for God and a healthy fear of how our sin will hurt us if we partake of it. There's not the slightest danger in saying that God's love is unconditional. He wasn't the enemy in the first place. Jesus came to save us from our sin and its destructive results. God's unconditional love is the only type of love that is powerful enough to win us at a heart level and inspire us to want to live differently!

"Love God and do as you please," Augustine said. But notice the first condition. "Love God!" If this condition is met, then you *can* do as you please, because your love for God has changed what you would be pleased to do.

Yes, He is able to keep us from falling, but in order for a child to ever learn to walk, run, and then sprint, the child must have an assurance that a fall will not jeopardize the love in his or her parents' hearts. Only when we feel that in God's heart it's OK when we fall will we have the assurance to risk the fall in order to learn how to walk.

Now we find Jesus relating to one of the very ones who has come to take Him away, a servant of the high priest and member of the mob. During this whole ordeal, Jesus never once concerned Himself with what was happening to Him; His only concern was the fate of others, even that of those who were about to inflict suffering upon Him.

"And one of them struck the slave of the high priest and cut off his right ear. But Jesus answered and said, 'Stop! No more of this.' And He touched his ear and healed him." (Luke 22:50, 51).

In the fray Peter had lashed out with his sword—trying to take off this servant's head. Ducking, the servant dodged the end of his life by a heartbeat but was not able to wholly avoid Peter's swing, losing an ear. Jesus abruptly put an end to the outburst. With no concern for Himself, He interposed between the mob and His disciples, commanding Peter to put away his sword. Stooping down, He picked up the servant's mangled ear and, while looking into this servant's eyes, paused. Everyone watched in breathless silence, waiting to see what would happen next. Never had this servant seen such love in any person's eyes. Encountering a love he didn't understand, he felt the touch of Jesus' hand on each side of His face and heard a whisper through his pain, "Don't be afraid. I've got you. Everything is going to be OK." Warmth filled the side of the servant's head, and reaching up, he realized that he had just been healed by the very man he came to murder. *Why? Why did He do this for me?* he likely asked himself. *And those eyes . . . those eyes.* Something began to awaken in that servant's self-centered heart, something he had never felt before.

Paul referred to this miraculous awakening, which is not reserved for just this servant, but for all who will believe what they find in the eyes of Jesus.

"The love of Christ compels me, having died for all, that those who live should henceforth no longer live for themselves but Him who died for them and rose again" (see 2 Cor. 5:14, 15).

Dear reader, can you feel it? Can you feel this love awakening something deep inside of you? "They spat in His face and beat Him with their fists; and others slapped Him" (Matt. 26:67). Throughout all of this, Satan was seeking to break the will of Jesus and to cause Him to loosen His grip on you. But love would not let go. Jesus settles all doubt. There is nothing we can do to God to make Him let go, to make Him stop loving us. He loves us, not because we are lovable, but because He is love. His kindness toward us is not because we are kind, but because He is. He is good to us, not because we are good, but because He is a beautiful, generous, good God who sincerely loves us.

Next we find ourselves looking at Peter. Here was one of Jesus' closest friends during His three years of ministry. He had been there since the beginning. And though in the most privileged of situations, Peter failed when Jesus needed him the most.

Having denied Jesus three times, with swearing and cursing to prove it, we pick up the story. "Immediately, while [Peter] was still speaking, a rooster crowed. The Lord turned and looked at Peter. And Peter remembered" (Luke 22: 60, 61).

As soon as Jesus heard the rooster crow, His attention was immediately diverted to the need of His friend Peter. This was in the very moments when Jesus' face was being spit upon and slapped, while blow after blow was felt from His accusers' fists. The rooster's caw captured Jesus' attention. He knew what Peter had just done. He knew the immense shame and regret that would soon overcome Peter. The matter was urgent—Peter must be found. There was no utter disbelief that Peter could have denied his friendship with Jesus so quickly and easily, no desire for recourse. He knew that Peter's spirit was willing, but also that Peter's flesh was weak. This failure, in the shadow of such commitment to the contrary,[2] was going to be too much for Peter to bear. Jesus urgently scanned the crowd; He must find him! Knowing He wouldn't be able to say anything, Jesus' only hope was to communicate to Peter what was in His heart using only the look in His eye.

"There he is! There's Peter!" The realization of what he had done had already begun to sink into Peter's heart. The guilt was mounting. Despair and self-disgust were taking their evil hold on Peter's heart. And then, out of nowhere, Peter saw those familiar eyes. Yet this time, there was something there he'd never seen with such intensity. What was Jesus so desperately trying to communicate to Peter? What did Peter encounter in the face of Jesus? No censure, no disappointment. Peter encountered the assurance of pardon in Jesus' fixed gaze. Jesus understood, had already forgiven him, and still loved him with a love much stronger than Peter's denial.

"Though you deny me Peter, I remain, forever *your friend*." How did Peter respond? Peter "went out and wept bitterly" (Matt. 26:75). These were tears not of guilt, but rather repentance. The goodness and forgiveness of this God had broken Peter's heart and awakened in him a change.[3]

Does this not strike at the heart of the thought that when we deny or rebel against God, He somehow takes vengeance on us? How many say, when faced with some hardship in their life, "Well, I guess God must be angry with me"? Or they ask, "What did I do to deserve this?" Is this really the way God responds to our shortcomings and failures? Or does He seek to free us from our guilt and shame, as He did with Peter, by reassuring us that He still loves us? When we sin, we don't need to be saved from God. We need to be saved from sin and the chain of events that we have now set in motion by our failure. God is not against you, dear reader. He is ever seeking to save you. He loves you. Do you believe this?

At Jesus' resurrection Peter was not forgotten. "Go tell the disciples" was the message, but then one in particular was singled out. "Don't forget to tell Peter."[4] Yes, Peter had made a terrible failure. But Jesus' greater concern was that Peter would know that his Friend still loved him. "Don't forget to tell Peter. Let him know especially."

All of Jesus' disciples had deserted Him that night. Yet this came as no surprise to Jesus. He knew it was going to happen before it did. "Then Jesus said to them, 'You will all fall away because of Me this night, for it is written, "I will strike down the shepherd, and the sheep of the flock shall be scattered." But after I have been raised, I will go ahead of you to Galilee'" (Matt 26:31, 32).

"Though you will forsake me, I will never forsake you." Jesus already knew, and had already forgiven them. What understanding and acceptance. What self-abandonment. Could this be what God is really like?

Next we find ourselves listening in on Jesus being interviewed by the Roman governor, Pilate. Pilate had the power to set Jesus free. Instead:

"Pilate then took Jesus and scourged Him" (John 19:1).

After Jesus' scourging, Pilate interceded for His release but, in a rude awakening, discovered the criminal accusation against Jesus: He, although a man, had claimed to be God. Raised a Roman under the influence of Greek mythology, Pilate had heard legends of how deities had, at other times in earth's history, taken human form and had walked this earth and interacted with humans. Could this man be a god? Fear began to seize Pilate's heart as he realized that there may be more to this case than he had previously judged.

"Therefore when Pilate heard this statement, he was even more afraid; and he entered into the Praetorium again and said to Jesus, 'Where are

You from?' But Jesus gave him no answer. So Pilate said to Him, 'You do not speak to me? Do You not know that I have authority to release You, and I have authority to crucify You?' Jesus answered, 'You would have no authority over Me, unless it had been given you from above; for this reason he who delivered Me to you has the greater sin'" (verses 8-11).

Look deeper at Jesus' answers to Pilate. What was He trying to do for Pilate? Pilate was feeling fear, which would later turn to guilt as the realization of what he had done settled in. At the very least he was anxious about his own well-being if this man standing before him really was a god. While knowing all of this about him, love for Pilate rose up in Jesus' heart. As He was being questioned, Jesus sought to lessen the guilt and fear that Pilate would encounter in the next few hours as the realization of what he had done sunk in. Jesus was seeking to lessen Pilate's guilt with the words "Those who handed Me over to you are more to blame than you, Pilate."

What is Jesus saying? Why is Jesus doing this? Let Pilate have it, Jesus! Lay the shame on thick! How could he abuse his judicial post to this extent and have an innocent man crucified? And not just any innocent man, but Jesus, the Son of God! Jesus came to lose it all, even for Pilate. Jesus genuinely loved Pilate and was desirous of saving him. Jesus also is desirous of saving us. What is it about God that Jesus would have us *see* in His interchange with Pilate? What do we learn about God's response to our sins through the window of His response to Pilate?

The God of the universe was standing before him, and Pilate was faced with a decision. Would he save Jesus at expense to himself, or save himself at expense to Jesus? If he should set Jesus free, he would possibly lose his position in that region because of the rebellion that would arise. So the decision became clear.

In a few short hours, on the cross, Jesus would be faced with a similar decision about Pilate. Should he save Pilate at eternal ruin to Himself, or save Himself at Pilate's eternal ruin? Jesus would choose to save Pilate, along with the entire world, at any cost to Himself. This same Pilate, who just hours previously had chosen to self-centeredly save himself at any cost to Jesus, would be the object of Christ's affection as He hung suspended between heaven and earth.

Today's Christian world says that if we do not repent, then ultimately God will torment us for ever and ever. I do believe the lost will suffer a final fate. But God is desperately engaging every agency of heaven to liberate us from the life-crushing guilt and shame that is inherent to our sin.

God is on *our* side, just as He was on Pilate's. We don't need to win Him. He is actively pursuing us, endeavoring to lessen, alleviate, and eradicate the guilt we feel. He knows that if we are not saved from underneath this weight, one day our life will be crushed out.

Again and again we find Jesus, in those closing moments of His life, intensely interested in the welfare and salvation of those who were crucifying Him instead of being concerned with what humanity was doing to Him. He was completely other-centered. The pure selflessness of God's noncondemning, forgiving love shone brighter and brighter with each new infliction. Even when pressed with as much suffering as can humanly be endured, God continued to love. He would not stop! We cannot change His mind and heart about us. Is this really how God feels toward us?

Along the way to Golgotha, the crucifixion site, we find Him again with complete disregard for Himself, concerned only for those around Him as He turned to face the train of weeping women behind Him.

"But Jesus turning to them said, 'Daughters of Jerusalem, stop weeping for Me, but weep for yourselves and for your children'" (Luke 23:28).

One of the most provocative events of Jesus' closing hours is what took place between Him and the thief on the cross. Countless sermons have been given and countless pages have been written on this interchange throughout Christian history. But do we believe what Jesus' exchange with this thief is telling us about how God thinks and feels toward us? Put yourself in the position of this thief while fully believing that this Being beside you is the God of this universe, being crucified for you.

"But the other criminal rebuked him. 'Don't you fear God . . . ? We are punished justly . . . But this man has done nothing wrong.' Then he said, 'Jesus, remember me when you come into your kingdom'" (verses 40–42, NIV).

"Jesus answered him, 'Today I tell you the truth, you will be with Me in paradise'" (verse 23, paraphrased).

No, Jesus, this is a thief! He's probably a murderer! And just like that, you're letting Him into Paradise? You're promising him he'll be there? No, Jesus, that's going too far. Here we must pause in silent meditation before this scene. No one else had stood up for Jesus. Not a disciple, friend, or relative had spoken one word defending Him in the past 24 hours, until these words spoken by a thief.

Why did he do it? We aren't told, but pay close attention to what the thief called Jesus. He called Him "Lord" (verse 42, KJV). What does this reveal? I don't know how, I don't know when, but something had awoken in the heart of this thief for Jesus. And even though there was nothing in it for him, he rushed to Jesus' defense. The only one who defended Jesus in the closing moments of His life was a criminal on death row. This has always bothered me. If I were there, would I have done differently?. Would I have done as Jesus' disciples did, or would I followed the example of the thief?

This thief stood up for Jesus when there was nothing in it for himself! In a few hours Jesus would be faced with this very decision for the entire world. Would He save us, even with nothing in it for Himself? What encouragement this thief must have given Jesus! The intended awakening to His love had worked for this one. My Savior was encouraged by a thief, when it should have been me! My heart breaks.

In those final moments Jesus would choose, in the face of eternal loss, to save me at any cost to Himself. Jesus, feeling as if He were saying goodbye to life forever, chose to save me when there was no heaven in it for Him. And whom do we have to thank? Certainly Jesus, but when I get there, I'm especially going to seek out that thief and thank him for doing what we should have done, for being the only one who stood up for our Savior, for being the one to evidence for Jesus that His love can change even the self-centered heart of a hardened criminal. Without this thief's encouragement, I shudder to think how much worse Jesus' mental questions and doubt would have been. I want to thank this thief for encouraging my Jesus. The thief had heard Jesus' call to this prodigal son. He had heard Jesus' love for him whispering, "Whatever you've done, whatever you've become, it doesn't matter to Me. Just come home." And what did the thief do? He came home.

"When they came to the place called The Skull, there they crucified Him. . . . But Jesus was saying, 'Father, forgive them; for they do not know what they are doing'" (Luke 23:33, 34).

What is this unstoppable thing in the heart of God? In this prayer we see it in full pristine clarity. We could not crush it. We could not quench it. We crucified it, but it would not die. What is it that we see here? We see the eternal, immortal, self-abandoning, self-sacrificing, noncondemning, unconditional, selfless love of our God.

The word "forgive" in this verse comes from the Greek word *aphiemi*. It does not refer to the violated party letting go of any ill feelings He may have toward the violators. God was already forgiving us in His heart even before Calvary. That's what Calvary was all about. Calvary was the exponent of the forgiveness that was already in the heart of God toward us. God was in Christ, forgiving the world. Notice Paul's words to the believers in Colossae.

"When you were dead in your transgressions and the uncircumcision of your flesh, He made you alive together with Him, having forgiven us all our transgressions, having canceled out the certificate of debt consisting of decrees against us, which was hostile to us; and He has taken it out of the way, having nailed it to the cross." (Col. 2:13, 14).

The whole purpose of the cross was to communicate to us that the charges have been dropped. When Jesus prayed this prayer in His darkest hour, He was praying for a change to be brought about in our psyches. He knew that our hearts would be almost wholly crushed when we, as a race, realized what we did to God that terrible day. And once again we find that Jesus was concerned only for us. His prayer was for removal of our guilt, a cleansing of our conscience. It was a prayer that we would not be tormented by our shame but that we would be set free. Jesus knew we didn't understand what part we were playing in His crucifixion, and that all too late the discovery of our sin would dawn upon our consciousness. When we would realize the result of our sin, Jesus was concerned that we would be crushed by the weight of that realization.

Jesus' prayer embraced the world, every person who ever lived or ever will live, from the beginning of time until the end. It embraces you, dear friend, whoever you are. Right now, whatever you have done, whatever you've become, you too can have psychological and emotional peace. The Father wants to cleanse your heart and mind of the guilt and shame of your past. He wants you to be at rest. Won't you surrender to Him and let that prayer of Jesus on your behalf be answered right now? Won't you stop right here, thank Him, and let the whole wicked business go? If you will, my dear friend, you will never be the same. Simply choose right now to believe that whatever you have done in your life, our God has *already forgiven you.*

We thought all along that Jesus was being punished by God for our sins. But we have now discovered that Jesus and God the Father are one, and that their oneness cannot be separated. The role of God at the cross was not punisher, but punished. God was in Christ! When we see Jesus, we see the Father! According to Isaiah, it wasn't the Father who was unleashing His wrath on Jesus. Look carefully at the words of Isaiah:

"He was despised and forsaken *of men*, a man of sorrows and acquainted with grief; and like one from whom *men hide their face* He was despised, and *we did not esteem Him.* Surely *our griefs* He Himself bore, and *our sorrows* He carried; *yet we ourselves esteemed Him stricken, smitten of God, and afflicted.* But He was pierced through *for our transgressions* ["rebellions" (New Jerusalem)], He was crushed *for our iniquities*; the chastening *for our well-being* fell upon Him, and by His scourging *we are healed*" (Isa. 53:3-5).

"He took the punishment by which we have peace" (verse 5, Basic English).

"Upon Him was the chastisement that brought us peace" (verse 5, ESV).

"Upon Him was the chastisement that makes us whole" (verse 5, NAB).

"The punishment that brought us peace was upon him" (verse 5, NIB).

"The punishment reconciling us fell on him" (verse 5, New Jerusalem).

There are two questions we need to answer in order to understand this passage. By whom was Jesus suffering and for what?

Jesus was not doing one thing at Calvary and the Father another. The Father was in Christ doing His work in His Son.[5] With this in mind, let's look at the passage more closely.

The passage states over and over by whom Jesus suffered:

"He was despised and forsaken *of men*."

"Like one from whom *men* hide their face."

"*We* did not esteem Him."

"He was despised [*by us*]."

"A man of sorrows and acquainted with grief." Whose sorrows and whose grief?

"Surely *our griefs* He Himself bore, and *our sorrows* He carried."

"*Yet we ourselves* esteemed Him stricken, smitten of God, and afflicted."

By whom did Jesus suffer? Clearly, it was by us.

For what did Jesus suffer? We did it, but God was using it and orchestrating it for a higher purpose, a purpose that many people, even today, do not understand. It was for the purpose of showing us His unstoppable love. Here Isaiah is focusing only on the physical aspects of the suffering of Jesus and begins to explain to us why Jesus must suffer physical violence at our hands.

Who pierced His hands and feet? We did.

Who crushed His body? We did.

Who punished, or chastised, Him? We did.

Who scourged Him? We did.

Notice the effect. By the scourging we inflicted on Him, we are healed. It does not say that God's anger is appeased, but that we are healed! We had transgressed, rebelled, and had become something He never intended—self-centered. In order to save us from the disastrous consequences, our condition required that Jesus must submit to as much hatred and violence as His human nature could endure. It was because of our "transgression," because of our "iniquities." He came to lose it all, so that we might "understand with [our hearts]" and be healed" (Matt. 13:15). He wanted us to *see*.

Peter, quoting from Isaiah, tells us:

"And while being reviled, He did not revile in return; while suffering, He uttered no threats . . . He Himself bore our sins in His body on the cross, so that we might die to sin and live to righteousness; for by His wounds you were healed" (1 Peter 2:23, 24).

The purpose of Jesus' sacrifice was that "we might die to sin [our self-centeredness] and live to righteousness [other-centeredness]." We are the ones who are healed from the effects of our transgression and iniquity. Look carefully at the phrase "He Himself bore our sins in His body on the cross." *The Bible in Basic English* translates it, "He took our sins on himself, giving his body to be nailed on the tree, so that we, being dead to sin, might have a new life in righteousness, and by his wounds we have been made well." We have been made whole again. By love, love has been awakened.

Simeon, a devout Jew present at Baby Jesus' Temple dedication, prophesied about the purpose of the cross: "To the end that thoughts from many hearts may be revealed" (Luke 2:35). Truly we begin to see the heart of the Father in the sufferings of Jesus. Jesus was showing us what is in God's heart toward all those who have sinned against Him. Rather than striking back, God turns the other cheek. He takes up the basin and the towel and seeks to save.

Calvary is shouting the words of the psalmist to us from the rooftops: "If You, Lord, should mark iniquities, O Lord, who could stand? But there is forgiveness with You" (Ps. 130:3, 4). Forgiveness? Could we not sum up all of Christ's actions on Calvary with this one word? Could this be what God is trying to have us understand? If we could truly grasp the forgiveness and love of our God revealed through the cross, it would liberate us psychologically and emotionally from the guilt produced by the past, and forever change our future by awakening in us a desire to live the rest of our days for something greater than ourselves—Him!

Dear reader, is this how you see God responding to your personal sins against Him? Or do you see Him ready to retaliate or punish you? Everything depends upon correct perception. What is your picture of God? How do you perceive His heart toward you—ill feelings or compassion? Jesus revealed to us how God responds when we violate Him on any level. Is Calvary your picture of God when you have fallen? This is the fundamental question that you must answer for right now and for eternity.

---

[1] The Greek word here for "forgiveness" is *aphesis*, which comes from the root word *aphiemi* meaning "a cleansing of guilt and shame from the violator's conscience."

[2] "But Peter said to Him, 'Even though all may fall away because of You, I will never fall away'" (Matt. 26:33).

[3] "Or do you think lightly of the riches of His kindness and tolerance and patience, not knowing that the kindness of God leads you to repentance?" (Rom. 2:4).

[4] "But go, tell His disciples and Peter" (Mark 16:7).

[5] "Do you not believe that I am in the Father, and the Father is in Me? The words that I say to you I do not speak on My own initiative, but the Father abiding in Me does His works" (John 14:10).

Chapter Seventeen

Love's Awakening

"Enemy-occupied territory—that is what this world is. Christianity is the story of how the rightful king has landed, you might say landed in disguise, and is calling us all to take part in a great campaign of sabotage."—C. S. LEWIS.

"Love is the basis of godliness. Whatever the profession, no man has pure love to God unless he has unselfish love for his brother. But we can never come into possession of this spirit by trying to love others. What is needed is the love of Christ in the heart. When self is merged in Christ, love springs forth spontaneously. The completeness of Christian character is attained when the impulse to help fills the heart and is revealed in the countenance."—E. G. WHITE.

"Let your light shine before men in such a way that they may see your good works, and glorify your Father who is in heaven."—JESUS (MATT. 5:16).

Again and again in Scripture the analogy of light and darkness is used. I believe God is seeking to communicate to us through the use of these two opposites. What is darkness? What is light? Many immediately say, "Oh, the darkness is sin!" With a little more thought, we will see that sin is in reality only the fruit, or result, of darkness. In order to discover the meaning of darkness, let's look at its opposite—light. What is light in Scripture? Jesus said that He is the light. He also said that He is the truth. If light is the Bible's symbol for truth, what is darkness? Lies. Just like darkness, the abounding lies around us keep us from being able to *see* the Father's true character.

Jesus also used this imagery when referring to us. He said that we, once imbued with God's love, would become the light of the world. We are to let our light shine forth so that others may see the good works we do and credit it to the Father of us all.

FINDING THE FATHER

The phrase "good works" has a very negative connotation for many. You see, good works have been manipulated out of God's people through fear of hell or hope of personal reward, either temporally (prosperity) or eternally (heaven).

Rarely have we seen the true purpose of good works. The good works that God's love brings out in our lives are not primarily about us. We have the privilege of being joined with Christ in showing to the world the truth about the nature of our heavenly Father. Consider the Bible's description of what our "good works" are to be.

"Owe nothing to anyone except to love one another; for he who loves his neighbor has fulfilled the law. For this, 'You shall not commit adultery, You shall not murder, You shall not steal, You shall not covet,' and if there is any other commandment, it is summed up in this saying, 'You shall love your neighbor as yourself.' Love does no wrong to a neighbor; therefore love is the fulfillment of the law" (Rom. 13:8, 9). "For the whole Law is fulfilled in one word, in the statement, 'You shall love your neighbor as yourself'" (Gal. 5:14). Even James, who is faithful to the statements about Abraham being justified by his works, stated that the law was about love.

"If, however, you are fulfilling the royal law according to the Scripture, 'You shall love your neighbor as yourself,' you are doing well" (James 2:8).

In each of these passages we begin to see that the Bible basis for all we do as Christians is love. This becomes alarming as you begin to see how far we have fallen from this ideal. How many times has Christianity been the source of bloodshed, crusades, murder, strife, and the division that is often found in local churches? Jesus spoke sharp words to the Pharisees.

"Woe to you, scribes and Pharisees, hypocrites! For you tithe mint and dill and cumin, [you're very religious, but . . .], and have neglected the weightier provisions of the law: justice and mercy and faithfulness; but these are the things you should have done without neglecting the others" (Matt. 23:23).

In Luke's Gospel, Jesus added, ". . . and yet disregard . . . the love of God . . ." (Luke 11:42).

We often pick various and sundry things that set us apart from others: diet, dress, style of worship music. But Jesus said that the primary characteristic identifying people who follow Jesus is the love they reveal in their relation to each other. "By this all men will know that you are *My disciples* [My followers], if you have love for one another" (John 13:35).

Jesus, through many illustrations, sought to communicate this foundational truth to those of His day.

"You are the salt of the earth; but if the salt has become tasteless, how can it be made salty again? It is no longer good for anything, except to be thrown out and trampled under foot by men" (Matt. 5:13).

In Jesus' day salt was harvested from the Dead Sea along with other white rocks that could not be distinguished from the salts. Their solution was simply to put all the white rocks in a cheesecloth. When preparing food, like soup, for example, those in the time of Christ would stir the cloth in the food until the salt had dissolved. After a period of time, all of the salt would dissolve, and the remaining gravel would be cast out and "trodden under foot of men" (verse 13, KJV).

What was Jesus saying to us in this parable? What does it mean for Christians to lose their salt? We may be doing much good in the name of Christ, but if we are not experiencing and exhibiting love, then it is all for nothing. We have gained nothing. Love is the centerpiece of all we do, flavoring all our actions.

Jesus also likened our relationships with one another to logs and splinters.

"Why do you look at the speck that is in your brother's eye, but do not notice the log that is in your own eye? Or how can you say to your brother, 'Let me take the speck out of your eye,' and behold, the log is in your own eye?" (Matt. 7:3, 4).

Notice the composite equality between a splinter and a log. They are both composed of the same material—wood! The only difference is their size.

God's attitude toward sinners is much different from His attitude toward sin. Again, God hates sin with a hatred as strong as death, but He loves the sinner with a love that is stronger than death. While God condemns sin, He convicts the sinner. Why does God condemn sin? Because sin is not simply breaking some rule, but an inherently harmful condition that sets in motion a chain of events that ultimately brings hurt to you and me, the objects of His affection.

We humans are quite the opposite. We love sin and hate sinners. In a religious setting this becomes subtle, but still true nonetheless. Many times, in order to look better to ourselves, we condemn those around us who are not living up to our expectations. When we imbibe this spirit of condemnation, we are embracing an un-Godlike, or ungodly, principle. It's inherently destructive, and quite the opposite of how God feels about, relates to, and helps sinners. Thus, the spirit of condemning sinners for their behavior is itself *sin*. It's ungodly! Yet notice the clincher. What is the size difference between the sin we see in others and the sin of condemning them for it? Their sin, when compared to our condemnation of them, is a splinter. Our condemnation of them for their sin, when compared to their actions, is equivalent to a two-by-four protruding from our eyes. Both are made of wood. Both are an ungodly way of living, but which is the greater sin according to Jesus? It's not the sin we condemn in others, but the spirit of condemnation that we find in ourselves.

Notice Paul's words: "And hope does not disappoint, because *the love of God* has been poured out within our hearts through the Holy Spirit who was given to us." (Rom. 5:5).

"But the fruit of the Spirit is *love*" (Gal. 5:22).

If the Holy Spirit is the root, love will be the fruit! Love is shed abroad in our hearts through the Holy Spirit. Love is the first characteristic listed in the fruit of the Spirit. That's right—love.

Could it be that the only difference between those serving God in name only and those who are truly following God just before He returns is the way they relate to other people, the way they love others?

Jesus tried to teach this to His followers. "Because lawlessness is increased, most people's love will grow cold. But the one who endures to the end, he will be saved" (Matt. 24:12, 13). What does "the one who endures" mean? While most people's love is waxing cold, those whose love endures to the end will be saved.

The prophetic book of Revelation reveals that in the end–times there will be Christians who, rather than winning people's worship through love, will be compelling it with threats of death. Why do they rely on force? Because they have lost the power of love. Their teachings, their experience, and their motives are devoid of love, and when the power of love has been lost, the only prevailing power is force.

"And it was given to him to give breath to the image of the beast, so that the image of the beast would even speak and cause as many as do not worship the image of the beast to be killed" (Rev. 13:15).

Jesus pointed us forward to this time as well.

"These things I have spoken to you so that you may be kept from stumbling. They will make you outcasts from the synagogue, but an hour is coming for everyone who kills you to think that he is offering service to

God. These things they will do because they have not known the Father or Me" (John 16:1–3).

Why is it that they will do such things? They do not know the Father or Jesus. John stated the same thing.

"The one who does not love *does not know God*, for God is love" (1 John 4:8).

"Beloved, now we are children of God, and it has not appeared as yet what we will be. We know that when He appears, we will be like Him, *because we will see Him just as He is*" (1 John 3:2).

"Beloved, let us love one another, for love is from God; and everyone who loves is born of God and *knows God*" (1 John 4:7).

The key is that if we don't understand God's love for us, we ourselves cannot love. Consequently we must resort to compelling others' behavior in religious matters. But if we know God, if we understand His love, His character, and who and what He is, we will understand that only by love can love be awakened. Love, therefore, becomes the driving power in all we say and do in our religion.

Love is the great centerpiece around which everything else clusters. The Bible states that there will be some in heaven who have never even heard the story of Calvary. They won't know what the holes in Jesus hands are all about.

"And one shall say unto him, What are these wounds in thine hands? Then he shall answer, Those with which I was wounded in the house of my friends" (Zech. 13:6, KJV).

I can't wait to listen to Jesus give a gospel presentation to one of these folks! But if that person has never heard the gospel story of the cross, how did he or she get there?

Sometimes the best way to answer a question is with another. Is Jesus more interested in people accepting Him in name or in principle? If someone has never even heard of Jesus, but through the influence of the Holy Spirit has accepted the great principle of heaven (unselfish love) into his or her life, has he or she not accepted Jesus even without knowing Him by that name?

The kingdom of heaven and the kingdom of Satan are opposites. Any service that is not done in love, even if it is done in "God's name," cannot be rendered to God. And no service done in accord with the principles of other-centered love can be rendered to Satan. One may never have heard the name of Jesus, but if that one accepts the principle of other-centered love as his or her way of life, he or she has accepted heaven's principles, has rejected Satan's, and is counted as a subject of God's kingdom. Truly love is the great centerpiece of Christianity around which all else revolves.

Let's see how this principle plays out in our life according to Jesus.

"But I say to you who hear, love your enemies, do good to those who hate you, bless those who curse you, pray for those who mistreat you. Whoever hits you on the cheek, offer him the other also; and whoever takes away your coat, do not withhold your shirt from him either. Give to everyone who asks of you, and whoever takes away what is yours, do not demand it back. Treat others the same way you want them to treat you. If you love those who love you, what credit is that to you? For even sinners love those who love them. If you do good to those who do good to you, what credit is that to you? For even sinners do the same. If you lend to those from whom you expect to receive, what credit is that to you? Even sinners lend to sinners in order to receive back the same amount. But love your enemies, and do good, and lend, expecting nothing in return; and your reward will be great, and you will be sons of the Most High; for He Himself is kind to ungrateful and evil men. Be merciful, just as your Father is merciful" (Luke 6:27–36).

This is more than a mere description of how Christ's followers are to live. It is a description of God Himself. The phrase "and you will be sons of the Most High" means that as children bear the resemblance of their parents, when we live according to this principle of other-centeredness, we will bear a resemblance to God. This truly describes godliness— Godlikeness.

This is the heart of the converting power of God's love. What if you were to choose to spend the rest of your life as God's enemy, hating Him, cursing Him daily, and mistreating Him and His followers? How would God treat you? Notice the question. It is not "How would sin treat you?" Sin is inherently destructive, and you would be setting in motion chains of events that would be self-destructive. But throughout all this, how would *God* treat you? He would love you still, He would do good to you, He would bless you and intercede continually for you.

"Wait!" you might say. What is it that would motivate you to serve God then? The motive for serving God far surpasses concern for ourselves. It is the sheer heart-touching force of God's unconditional kindness, His extreme generosity, even if He gets nothing in return. By this type of love, and this type of love only, is a reciprocating love awakened. Even if we do not serve God, He will continue to give us light and life, seeking by His love to win us from Satan's service.

Read it again from Matthew's Gospel.

"But I say to you, love your enemies and pray for those who persecute you, so that you may be sons of your Father who is in heaven; for He causes His sun to rise on the evil and the good, and sends rain on the righteous and the unrighteous" (Matt. 5:44, 45).

After Jesus was resurrected and returned to heaven, His disciples, now called apostles, understood the "even if you get nothing back" principle of God's love for us. You'll see it over and over in their lives. Stephen's dying prayer that God would not hold the religious leaders' unjust stoning of him against them was one example. And notice this principle's power to change lives.[1]

Paul, at that time called Saul, was there, holding the coats of those stoning Stephen. Paul had been spending his time persecuting followers of Jesus, thinking he was doing God a favor. Soon afterward, on the road to Damascus, Paul encountered the truth that He was actually fighting against God, but also discovered the light of God's amazing forgiveness and unconditional kindness.

This principle became part and parcel of the fabric of Paul's treatment of others. It's called disinterested benevolence, benevolence with no interest in what's in it for yourself.

We pick up Paul's life years later as He and his fellow missionary Silas sat in a Roman prison cell. They'd been beaten, bruised, bloodied, and then thrown into a jail cell. They had been poorly treated by the jailer, but nonetheless were both singing praises. This was more than Paul and Silas simply trying to keep their spirits up. They were truly rejoicing.

When someone mistreats you in a small way and you love that person back regardless, the revelation of your unconditional love for him or her in return is small, not having been tested much. But when someone significantly mistreats you and you respond with unaffected love, the revelation of that unconditional love is very significant. You see, the depth of love revealed is relative to the amount of suffering inflicted. Or in other words, the depth of love is revealed to the degree by which it is tested. As a side note, this is why Calvary is such a powerful revelation of God's love for humanity. Look at how we were treating Him and how He responded. When humanity exhausted its enmity against God, then and only then did we begin to comprehend the unconditional love of our Maker in return. We could not break His will; He would love us with reckless abandon regardless of and despite our treatment of Him.

Now back to our story. Paul and Silas were rejoicing in their sufferings because the sufferings created the potential to show greater love than they had ever been privileged to reveal before. This is the great passion of the followers of Jesus, to show His love to the world in crystal–clear clarity, regardless of the cost. This is what it means to share in the sufferings of Christ—to share in the revelation of Calvary-like suffering for the purpose of revealing the Father.[2]

Follow closely the response of the jailer in this story. We'll start from the very beginning.

"The crowd rose up together against them, and the chief magistrates tore their robes off them and proceeded to order them to be beaten with rods. When they had struck them with many blows, they threw them into prison, commanding the jailer to guard them securely; and he, having received such a command, threw them into the inner prison and fastened their feet in the stocks. But about midnight Paul and Silas were praying and singing hymns of praise to God, and the prisoners were listening to them; and suddenly there came a great earthquake, so that the foundations of the prison house were shaken; and immediately all the doors were opened and everyone's chains were unfastened. When the jailer awoke and saw the prison doors opened, he drew his sword and was about to kill himself, supposing that the prisoners had escaped. But Paul cried out with a loud voice, saying, 'Do not harm yourself, for we are all here!' And he called for lights and rushed in, and trembling with fear he fell down before Paul and Silas, and after he brought them out, he said, "Sirs, what must I do to be saved?" (Acts 16:22–30).

The jailer, thinking they had escaped, raised his sword to his chest. He knew the penalty if prisoners escaped on his watch. The jailer decided that it was better to die by his own hands than by the hands of his superiors. Paul stepped out of the shadows and shouted to the jailer, "Wait! Stop! I am a Roman by birth, and I know that if we depart this evening, your life will be in jeopardy. So even though you have unjustly beaten us, bruised and bloodied us, thrown us into the inmost parts of the prison, fastened us in stocks that have caused our joints and ankles to swell in pain," Paul, now with tears of love for the jailer in his eyes, took a deep breath for the punch line, "we are willing to go back into that jail cell and rot, if it means your life is preserved!" What love! What a revelation to the jailer. And how did the jailer respond? With solemnity and gratitude in his voice, he replied reverently, "Sirs, what must I do to be saved?"

Over and over people ask me why there is not more evangelistic efficiency in Christianity today. I don't believe that the pull of the world has gotten stronger. There is nothing new under the sun. Rather, could it be that Christians are failing miserably to reveal the self-abandoning love of God in their treatment of others? Have they abandoned the love that gives such power to the message?

I believe with all my heart that this is the reason God sent the earthquake to set Paul and Silas free. He knew their hearts. He knew they would not bolt like most of us, but would be more concerned for the jailer than themselves and stay. God was using them to show His love for the jailer. Could this also be the reason there is not more suffering in North America by Christians? Would we respond to our persecutors as Paul and Silas did? Certainly there is persecution in other places, but if the current climate of tolerance toward Christians in North America changed, how many would retaliate rather than take the opportunity to show Calvary-quality love?

"For you have been called for this purpose, since Christ also suffered for you, leaving you an example for you to follow in His steps . . . ; and while being reviled, He did not revile in return; while suffering, He uttered no threats" (1 Peter 2:21–23).

We see this principle revealed over and over in the lives of many of those who have followed Christ fully. Understanding and believing His great love for them awoke a love response to the great Lover of their soul. This love included those around them, whom God loves just as much.

Look at how Paul felt toward the religious leaders who were persecuting him, wishing for and working for his death.

"I am telling the truth in Christ, I am not lying, my conscience testifies with me in the Holy Spirit, that I have great sorrow and unceasing grief in my heart. For I could wish that I myself were accursed, separated from Christ for the sake of my brethren, my kinsmen according to the flesh" (Rom. 9:1–3).

The Greek word here for "accursed" is *anathema*. It means "cut off from God forever." Paul was stating that even though these Jewish brethren of his wanted him dead, he would nonetheless gladly give up his place in heaven for them if it meant they could be there. What incomprehensible love!

We see this love in Moses' life as well, in his prayer for the children of Israel who were the source of his many heartbreaks and near nervous breakdowns. When they were in jeopardy, Moses prayed, "But now, if You will, forgive their sin—and if not, please blot me out from Your book which You have written!" (Ex. 32:32).

Moses too was saying that if it were possible, he would give up his place in God's kingdom if that's what it would take for Israel to be saved.

Stop right now, right here, for a moment. I want you to picture in your mind the person on this planet whom you like the least. What would it take for you to be willing to give up your place in heaven for this person, if that's what it took for him or her to be there? This willingness is how God wants us to feel toward our enemies. Speaking of the suffering that Christ went through at Calvary and the illuminating revelation of God's love through that suffering, Paul states, "For God, who said, 'Light shall shine out of darkness,' is the One who has shone in our hearts to give the Light of the knowledge of the glory of God in the face of Christ. But we have this treasure in earthen vessels" (2 Cor. 4:6, 7). Did you catch Paul's meaning in his last phrase? The same light, or revelation of God, the same "treasure" that shone through Christ on Calvary, God wants to reveal through our earthen vessels as well. We may be only jars of clay, but God wants to reveal His love through us in the same way He revealed it through His Son.

However, we must always remember that we cannot love others like this by trying to love them. Rather, we need to encounter the heart of God for us. We need to encounter God's love for ourselves, and His love will awaken in us love back toward Him and the others around us. We need a clear understanding and belief in God's love for us in our hearts. Only this will awaken true love in us, even for our enemies.

In the Bible phrase found in 1 John 4:19, "We love Him because He first loved us" (NKJV), we must note that in the original Greek language, it does not say that we love Him, but simply that we *love*. God's love awakens love in us back not only toward Him but toward all!

Once again, Jesus said clearly, "Truly, truly, I say to you, the Son can do nothing of Himself, unless it is something He sees the Father doing; for whatever the Father does, these things the Son also does in like manner" (John 5:19). And just as Jesus could love only to the extent that He saw and understood His Father's love, so that we too can love only as we see the Father's love for us.

This is a basic principle. We will treat others only as well as we perceive God to be treating us. If we believe God condemns us for our sin, then we will naturally struggle with tendencies to condemn others for their sin. But if we believe God loves us unconditionally and is seeking to save us from our self-destructive ways, then this attitude of compassion and a desire to redeem those around us will be found in our hearts toward them as well. We, like Jesus, can do only as we see.

God condemns our wrong actions, not we who do those actions. He convicts us, but He does not condemn us. If we think God condemns us for our wrong actions, then when we see others engaging in activities we believe are wrong, we will condemn them as well.

John, looking into the future, saw a group following the principles of other-centered love toward their persecutors.

"Then I looked, and behold, the Lamb was standing on Mount Zion, and with Him one hundred and forty-four thousand, having His name and the name of His Father written on their foreheads. . . . These are the ones who follow the Lamb wherever He goes" (Rev. 14:1–4).

Why do they do exactly as the Lamb? Because they see what the Lamb sees. Notice that they have the Father's name written on their foreheads. Why is this significant? As in several Bible instances, a person's name is descriptive of what the person is like. The Father's name indicates His character, or what He is like. These 144,000 have the Father's name written in their foreheads. They, in an unshakable way, have been sealed in their understanding of God the Father's character. They know, perceive, and understand what He is truly like and so they naturally follow His actions.

Jesus said, "Truly, truly, I say to you, he who believes in Me, the works that I do, he will do also; and greater works than these he will do; because I go to the Father" (John 14:12). Paul speaks of this principle as well, that we are changed into the same image we see. "But we all, with unveiled face, beholding as in a mirror the glory of the Lord, are being transformed into the same image from glory to glory, just as from the Lord, the Spirit" (2 Cor. 3:18). This transformation is accomplished not through our efforts, or through our trying to be like God, but rather through something much more powerful.

"For in Christ Jesus neither circumcision nor uncircumcision means anything, but faith working through love" (Gal. 5:6).

In religious circles some argue that we are saved by faith alone. Others insist that we are saved by faith and works. Should we focus only on having faith, or should we focus on improving our works? In the above verse Paul says that there are three key ingredients for our lives: (1) faith, (2) works, and (3) love. Love is not just an addition to the list but a unifying factor. Love brings the ingredients together! When we see God's love, faith responds and goes to work. We are saved by God's love, through our faith, which goes to work revealing this love in our lives. Where our eyes need to be focused, then, is on God's love for us, for love produces faith and faith produces works. If our focus is surely fixed on God's love, we will just as surely experience both faith and good works (disinterested benevolence).

"What shall we say then? That Gentiles, who did not pursue righteousness, attained righteousness, even the righteousness which is by faith; but Israel, pursuing a law of righteousness, did not arrive at that law. Why? Because they did not pursue it by faith, but as though it were by works. They stumbled over the stumbling stone" (Rom. 9:30–32).

Why did they not experience the righteousness they desired? Because they focused on producing this love by their own best efforts. Others did attain it, but notice that these were not seeking it. The implication is that although they were not focusing on being righteous, they attained it through faith, and faith comes as a response to an encounter with God's love.

I want to mention some characteristics of faith that many people overlook. There is a certain type of belief that is cerebral. It is an intellectual assent to known facts that stimulates our intellect but leaves our hearts largely unaffected. Demons are experts in this type of belief. "You believe that God is one. You do well; the demons also believe, and shudder" (James 2:19).

But the faith through which we are saved (not *by*, but *through*) is not simply an intellectual assent to the fact that there is a God and He has a Son named Jesus; rather, it is a heart–level response to His love for us. Notice that believing, according to Scripture, is not an intellectual response but something we do with our hearts.

"And He said to them, 'O foolish men and *slow of heart to believe* in all that the prophets have spoken!'" (Luke 24:25).

"And Philip said, 'If you *believe with all your heart*, you may.' And he answered and said, 'I believe that Jesus Christ is the Son of God'" (Acts 8:37).

"For *with the heart a person believes*, resulting in righteousness, and with the mouth he confesses, resulting in salvation" (Rom. 10:10).

This makes perfect sense when you understand that faith is our response to God's love for us. God's love passes through our intellect, but it doesn't stop there! It goes on further and touches our heart. This heartfelt, deeply appreciative gratitude that makes you want to love Him back at a heart level is what the Bible calls *faith!* And this can come about only as a response to seeing how much He loves us![3] This is precisely why Paul's greatest concern for those to whom he ministered was that they would encounter God's extravagant love for them.

"For this reason I bow my knees before the Father, from whom every family in heaven and on earth derives its name, that He would grant you, according to the riches of His glory, to be strengthened with power through His Spirit in the inner man, so that Christ may dwell in your hearts through faith; and that you, being rooted and grounded in love, may be able to comprehend with all the saints what is the breadth and length and height and depth, and to know the love of Christ which surpasses knowledge, that you may be filled up to all the fullness of God" (Eph. 3:14-19).

John repeats this principle of doing what we see, or loving because we are loved. "Beloved, let us love one another, for love is from God; and everyone who loves is born of God and knows God. The one who does not love does not know God, for God is love" (1 John 4:7, 8). We now begin to love, period! An encounter with God's love awakens in us an other-centered love for all with whom we come in contact. We simply love, because He first loved us!

My prayer for you, dear friend, is that you will make God's love for you and this world the paramount passion of your life. May understanding it be your quest. May the truth of it be your message. May encountering His love be your focus and intent for yourself and for all around you. May His love dictate the methods you use in sharing it. The day is coming when all will know Him, from the least to the greatest. Does your heart long for this living, viable, other–centered, heart-to-ground, love relationship with your God? Then put all else aside. Do not avert your gaze. Fix your heart on His. "Believe not God is in your heart, child, but rather, that you are in the heart of God." And let the awakening begin.

If I speak with human eloquence and angelic ecstasy but don't love,
I'm nothing but the creaking of a rusty gate.
If I speak God's Word with power, revealing all his mysteries

and making everything plain as day,
and if I have faith that says to a mountain, "Jump," and it jumps,
but I don't love, I'm nothing.
If I give everything I own to the poor
and even go to the stake to be burned as a martyr,
but I don't love, I've gotten nowhere.
So, no matter what I say, what I believe, and what I do,
I'm bankrupt without love.

Love never gives up.
Love cares more for others than for self.
Love doesn't want what it doesn't have.
Love doesn't strut,
Doesn't have a swelled head,
Doesn't force itself on others,
Isn't always "me first,"
Doesn't fly off the handle,
Doesn't keep score of the sins of others,
Doesn't revel when others grovel,
Takes pleasure in the flowering of truth,
Puts up with anything,
Trusts God always,
Always looks for the best,
Never looks back,
But keeps going to the end.

Love never dies.
Inspired speech will be over some day;
praying in tongues will end;
understanding will reach its limit.
We know only a portion of the truth, and what we say about God is
always incomplete.
But when the Complete arrives, our incompletes will be canceled.
When I was an infant at my mother's breast, I gurgled and cooed like
any infant.
When I grew up, I left those infant ways for good.
We don't yet see things clearly. We're squinting in a fog, peering
through a mist.

But it won't be long before the weather clears and the sun shines bright!
We'll see it all then, see it all as clearly as God sees us,
knowing him directly just as he knows us!
But for right now, until that completeness,
we have three things to do to lead us toward that consummation:
Trust steadily in God, hope unswervingly, love extravagantly.
And the best of the three is love.

—1 Corinthians 13, Message

See! The winter is past; the rains are over and gone.
Flowers appear on the earth; the season of singing has come.

—Song of Songs 2:11, 12, NIV

[1] "They went on stoning Stephen as he called on the Lord and said, 'Lord Jesus, receive my spirit!' Then falling on his knees, he cried out with a loud voice, 'Lord, do not hold this sin against them!' Having said this, he fell asleep" (Acts 7:59, 60).

[2] "But to the degree that you share the sufferings of Christ, keep on rejoicing, so that also at the revelation of His glory you may rejoice with exultation" (1 Peter 4:13).

[3] "We love, because He first loved us" (1 John 4:19).

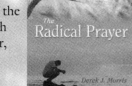

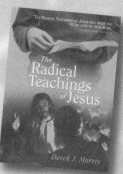

BOOKS TO ENRICH YOUR RELATIONSHIP WITH JESUS

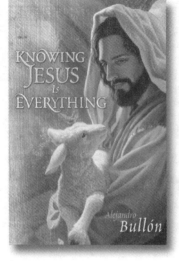

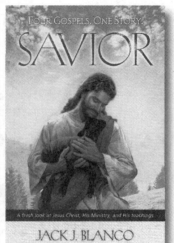

Knowing Jesus Is Everything

The Christian life is too difficult—if you don't know Jesus personally. No matter what you do (or don't do), you don't stand a chance without Him. Alejandro Bullón offers guidance for pursuing a genuine friendship with Jesus. 978-0-8280-2381-8

Savior

You've read the greatest story ever told—but never quite like this. Written in modern language without the disjointed interruption of chapter or verse, Jack Blanco merges the four Gospel accounts into one fresh, unified narrative. This is the timeless, captivating story of Jesus, our Savior. 978-0-8127-0469-3

Revelation's Great Love Story

Larry Lichtenwalter explores the final book of the Bible and unveils a side of Revelation that is seldom portrayed: Christ's passionate love for humanity. Open your eyes to the extraordinary love of our Savior for His rebellious, undeserving children—and the incredible reasons we can love Him in return. 978-0-8127-0460-0

3 Ways to Shop
- Visit your local Adventist Book Center®
- Call 1-800-765-6955
- Order online at www.AdventistBookCenter.com